English in Focus: Social Studies

ENGLISH IN FOCUS

Series Editors: J.P.B. ALLEN and H.G. WIDDOWSON

Physical Science   J.P.B. Allen and H.G. Widdowson*
Mechanical Engineering   Eric H. Glendinning*
Workshop Practice   Alan Mountford*
Basic Medical Science   Joan Maclean*
Education   Elizabeth Laird
Agriculture   Alan Mountford
Social Studies   J.P.B. Allen and H.G. Widdowson
Biological Science   Ian Pearson
Electrical Engineering and Electronics   Eric H. Glendinning

*Advisory Editor: RONALD MACKIN

ENGLISH IN FOCUS

English in Social Studies

J. P. B. ALLEN

H. G. WIDDOWSON

OXFORD UNIVERSITY PRESS

Oxford University Press, Walton Street, Oxford OX2 6DP

LONDON GLASGOW NEW YORK TORONTO
DELHI BOMBAY CALCUTTA MADRAS KARACHI
KUALA LUMPUR SINGAPORE HONG KONG TOKYO
NAIROBI DAR ES SALAAM CAPE TOWN SALISBURY
MELBOURNE AUCKLAND

and associates in

BEIRUT BERLIN IBADAN MEXICO CITY NICOSIA

ISBN 0 19 437518 8 (Student's Book)
ISBN 0 19 437509 9 (Teacher's Edition)
©Oxford University Press 1978

First published 1978
Second impression 1982

PRINTED IN HONG KONG

Contents

Unit 3 Social learning

Unit 4 Roles

Acknowledgements

The authors and publishers are grateful to the owners of copyright material used in the preparation of this book.

The population diagrams in Unit 5 are based on those in Paul R. Ehrlich and Anne H. Ehrlich (1972) *Population, Resources, Environment: Issues in Human Ecology*, second edition, San Francisco, W. H. Freeman and Company, and the census diagrams in Unit 6 on figures in E. J. B. Rose and others (1969) *Colour and Citizenship*, London, Institute of Race Relations and Oxford University Press, by permission of the publishers. The material on the history of urban development in Unit 7 is derived from R. E. Dickinson (1962) *The West European City*, London, Routledge and Kegan Paul. The texts in Unit 8 and its sketchmaps are based on or directly quoted from Colin Buchanan (1963) *Traffic in Towns*, London, Her Majesty's Stationery Office, by permission of the Controller.

The authors would like to thank Rosemary Johnson of the Department of Sociology, University of Edinburgh, for her comments on an early draft of the manuscript.

Introduction

The aim of this book is to develop a basic knowledge of how English is used for communication in dealing with topics in social studies. It is intended for students who already know how to handle the common English sentence patterns but who need to learn how these patterns are used to convey information and to conduct coherent discussion.

The exercises direct the student's attention to certain features of English which are commonly used in the social sciences. The aim is to provide the student with a strategy for reading more difficult texts in this subject area and to prepare him for making effective use of English in his own writing.

Although the emphasis is on English as a medium of expression for communicating ideas about the social sciences, the basic elements of the language have not been neglected. Pattern practice is provided, particularly in the use of language and guided writing sections of each unit, but this kind of work is always presented in relation to a communicative context and not simply as an exercise in making sentences for their own sake.

This book does not aim at teaching the subject-matter of the social sciences, and it does not aim at teaching grammatical structures and vocabulary as such. Its purpose is to show how language is used as a medium for social studies and so to give students a grounding in one particular set of communication skills in English.

1 Kinship and the family

I READING AND COMPREHENSION

NOTE *The reading passage at the beginning of each unit will be interrupted by certain statements printed in italics. The learner is required to assess whether these are true or false in the light of his understanding of the passage up to this point.*

[1]Most social anthropologists recognize the family as a basic social unit. [2]In its most elementary form it may be defined as a group consisting of a man and a woman and their children living together in one home. [3]Such a domestic group is known as a nuclear family. [4]It is usually established by means of a formal contract of marriage, but a contract of this kind is not a necessary condition for a nuclear family to exist. [5]It can also be said to exist when a couple and their offspring share a common residence, whether the couple is married or not. [6]That is to say, a family may exist even when the relationship between the man and the woman is one of concubinage rather than one of marriage.

Study the following statements carefully and write down whether they are true or not true according to the information expressed above. Then complete the solutions at the end of the passage by referring to the sentences indicated in brackets.* When the solutions are complete, you will be able to check your answers to the comprehension questions.

(a) *A nuclear family is a couple and their offspring sharing a common residence.*
(b) *A nuclear family is established by marriage.*

[7]Although we can, in general, define the nuclear family as a couple and their children living within the same residential boundary, we must recognize that such a definition is in fact a generalization which may not hold true in particular instances. [8]Sometimes a nuclear family is incomplete in that one

---

* Note that the completion may sometimes require the insertion of one word and sometimes of more than one. The following symbols are used in the solutions:
  i.e.   that is to say
  e.g.   for example
  =   equals, means the same as
  ∴   therefore

spouse is absent from the household. [9]When a family is incomplete it is usually the man rather than the woman who is away from home. [10]Such a situation may be the result of social convention. [11]For example, among the Ashanti, a tribe living in Ghana, spouses continue to reside with their own kin after marriage and do not live together as husband and wife. [12]On the other hand, a nuclear family may be incomplete by reason of economic necessity. [13]Sometimes, for example, a man has to leave his family to work in another part of the country or in a different country altogether. [14]This is the case with many workers in South Africa and with foreign workers in France and Germany.

(c)   *In an incomplete nuclear family it is the man who is absent from the household.*

(d)   *The man's absence is caused by economic necessity.*

[15]The nuclear family may be extended by the addition of other people living within the same residential boundary. [16]So far we have been assuming that the family is always based on monogamous marriage; that is to say, that it has only one man and one woman living together as husband and wife. [17]But monogamy is only one form of marriage. [18]In societies where polygamy is practised the family will, of course, include more than two spouses. [19]In the case of polygyny, it will include one husband and more than one wife, and in the case of polyandry it will include one wife and more than one husband. [20]In a polygynous society, therefore, the nuclear family will be extended by the addition of one or more wives and in polyandrous societies it will be extended by the addition of one or more husbands.

(e)   *In some families there are more than two spouses.*

(f)   *In polygynous societies, the nuclear families include more than one husband.*

[21]In both monogamous and polygamous societies, families may also be extended by the addition of related or non-related people. [22]In some, for example, people like servants and workmen live with the family as members of the household. [23]Again, one often finds that families are extended by the addition of consanguineal relatives, or kin, of one or more of the marriage partners, like brothers, sisters, fathers, grandfathers and so on. [24]Affinal relatives like brothers-in-law, sisters-in-law and so on may also become members of the family and share a common residence with the brother or sister of their spouses.

SOLUTIONS

Complete the following statements by referring to the sentences of the passage which are indicated in brackets. Note that sometimes more than one word is required.

(a) People who live together in one home are people who . . . (5). A man and a woman and their children sharing a common residence is a . . . (3) which is known as a nuclear family.

i.e. A . . . (5) and their . . . (5) sharing a common residence are known as a nuclear family.

= *A nuclear ·family is a couple and their offspring sharing a common residence.*

(b) A nuclear family is . . . (4) established by marriage.

but A family may exist even when . . . (5) is not married.

∴ Although a nuclear family is *usually* established by marriage, it can also be established by concubinage.

(c) In a nuclear family which is . . . (8), either the man or the woman is away from home.

i.e. One of the . . . (8) is . . . (8).
The spouse who is absent from the household is . . . (9) the man.

i.e. In an incomplete nuclear family it is the man who is *usually* absent from the household.

(d) The man is . . . (8) away because of . . . (12).

i.e. His absence *may* be caused by economic necessity.
The man is . . . (8) absent because of . . . (10).

i.e. His absence may also be caused by social convention.

∴ The man's absence may be caused by economic necessity *or* social convention.

(e) In a . . . (16) marriage there are two people living together as husband and wife.

but Not all marriages are . . . (16).

i.e. Not all families have only two . . . (18).

i.e. *In some families there are more than two spouses.*

(f) In a society where polygyny is practised the nuclear family includes more than one . . . (19).

= In polygynous societies, the nuclear families include more than one *wife.*

EXERCISE A   *Meaning assessment*

Refer to the passage and

(a) decide whether the following statements are true or false according to the passage, and

(b) write out the true statement which expresses the most central idea.

Paragraph 1

1. A nuclear family is always established by marriage.

2. A nuclear family is defined by common residence.
3. A nuclear family is a domestic group.

Paragraph 2
1. Ashanti husbands do not live with their wives.
2. Foreign workers in France are absent from their families because of social convention.
3. Sometimes a man has to leave his family to find work away from home.
4. Nuclear families are sometimes incomplete for one reason or another.

Paragraph 3
1. Nuclear families are monogamous.
2. There are two wives in polygamous homes.
3. In polygamous societies there are more than two spouses in the family.
4. In a polyandrous society a man may be married to more than one wife.

Paragraph 4
1. Kin are consanguineal relatives.
2. Sisters-in-law are kin.
3. In some societies relatives of the spouses may become members of the family.
4. Workmen sometimes become members of the household.

EXERCISE B   *Contextual reference*

Refer to the relevant contexts in the reading passage and replace or expand the expressions printed in italics with expressions which make the meaning clear. For example:

> *It* can also be said to exist when a couple and their offspring share a common residence, whether the couple is married or not. (5)
>
> A NUCLEAR FAMILY can also be said to exist when a man and a woman and their offspring share a common residence, whether the couple is married or not.

1. In its most elementary form *it* may be defined as a group consisting of a man and woman and their children living together in one home. (2)
2. *Such a domestic group* is known as a nuclear family. (3)
3. *A contract of this kind* is not a necessary condition for a nuclear family to exist. (4)
4. *Such a definition* is a generalization which may not always hold true in particular instances. (7)
5. *Such a situation* may be the result of social convention. (10)
6. In the case of polygyny, *it* will include one husband and more than one wife and in the case of polyandry *it* will include one wife and more than one husband. (19)

7. In polyandrous societies, *it* will be extended by the addition of one or more husbands. (20)
8. In *some*, people like servants live with the family as members of the household. (22)

EXERCISE C *Summary*

Arrange the final statements in the Solutions and put them together with the following statements to make a summary of the reading passage. Note: the statements are not in the right order.

1. Again, in some societies the family will be extended to include kin relatives and relatives by marriage.
2. A nuclear family is not always complete.
3. In the case of a polyandrous society, on the other hand, the nuclear family is extended by the addition of one or more husband.
4. In such societies, therefore, both consanguineal and affinal relatives may become members of the family.

II   USE OF LANGUAGE

EXERCISE D   *Definitions*

Write out definitions by combining expressions in Column I with appropriate expressions in Column II. For example:

I(a)+II(d)
A nuclear family is a group consisting of a man and a woman and their offspring sharing a common residence.

I	II
(a) a nuclear family	the relationship of a man and woman living together outside marriage
(b) monogamy	a nuclear family in which one spouse is absent from the household
(c) polygamy	the marriage of one man with more than one wife
(d) polygyny	a group consisting of a man and woman and their offspring sharing a common residence
(e) polyandry	people who are related by marriage

I	II
(f) consanguineal relatives	the marriage of one woman with more than one husband
(g) affinal relatives	the marriage of one man with one woman
(h) a spouse	people who are related by birth
(i) concubinage	the marriage of more than two spouses
(j) an incomplete nuclear family	a partner in marriage

EXERCISE E   *Generalizations and qualifications*

The following statements are *generalizations*:

   (i) Social anthropologists recognize the family as a basic social unit.
   (ii) A nuclear family is established by means of a formal contract of marriage.

Statement (i) means that *all* social anthropologists recognize . . .
   OR Social anthropologists *always* recognize . . .
Statement (ii) means that *all* nuclear families are established . . .
   OR Nuclear families are *always* established . . .

   Generalizations can be qualified. For example:

   (iii) *Some/many/most* social anthropologists recognize the family as a basic family unit.
   (iv) A nuclear family is *sometimes/often/usually* established by means of a formal contract of marriage.

Statement (iii) is a qualification of (i).
Statement (iv) is a qualification of (ii).

   Study the following table:

	Degrees of generalization	
I	all	always
II	most	usually generally
III	many	often frequently
IV	some	sometimes
V	few	seldom rarely

Qualify the following generalizations where necessary by using the appropriate expressions from each column. For example:

A nuclear family is established by means of a formal contract of marriage.
Most nuclear families are established by a formal contract of marriage.
A nuclear family is *usually* established by means of a formal contract of marriage.
OR
Nuclear families are *usually* established by a formal contract of marriage.

1. Ashanti husbands live apart from their wives.
2. Families are incomplete because the husband has to leave his family to work in another part of the country.
3. A nuclear family is established by concubinage.
4. A polygynous family consists of one husband and more than one wife.
5. Families are extended by the addition of consanguineal relatives.
6. Families are incomplete because the wife is absent from home.
7. In other societies distinctions are made between relatives which in English-speaking societies are grouped together under the same term.
8. In other societies, people like servants and workmen live with the family as members of the household.
9. Other societies recognize ties of kinship and affinity with people whom we in Western Europe would not regard as relatives at all.

EXERCISE F *Information transfer: definitions and descriptions*

The following diagram conveys the same information as the statement below it.

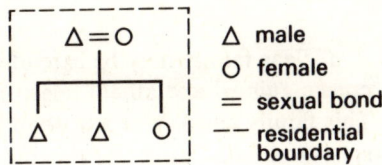

△ male
○ female
= sexual bond
-- residential boundary

(a) *Definition* A nuclear family is a group consisting of a man and a woman and their offspring sharing a common residence.
(b) *Description* This is a nuclear family consisting of a man and a woman, their two sons and one daughter.

1. Draw a diagram to correspond with the following definition and description:

   (a) *Definition* A polygynous family is a group consisting of one man and more than one woman and their offspring sharing a common residence.

(b) *Description* This is a polygynous family consisting of one man and two women, two sons of the man and one woman and one son and two daughters of the second woman.

2. Write a definition and a description based on the following diagram:

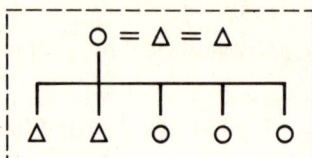

```
 _____
|         O = Δ = Δ            |
|         |                   |
|     ┌───┼───┬───┬───┐       |
|     Δ   Δ   O   O   O       |
|_____|
```

EXERCISE G   *Information transfer: generalizations and descriptions*

The following diagram can serve as a basis for the generalization and the description which appear below it:

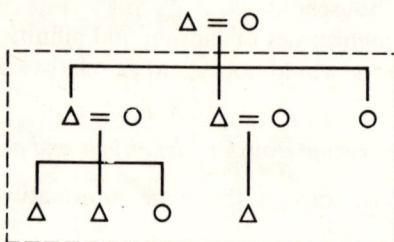

```
              Δ = O
 _____
|     ┌────────┼────────┐         |
|   Δ = O    Δ = O       O        |
|   |          |                  |
| ┌─┼─┐        |                  |
| Δ  Δ  O      Δ                  |
|_____|
```

(a) *Generalization* A nuclear family may be extended by the addition of consanguineal and affinal relatives.

(b) *Description*   This family consists of a husband and wife, their two sons and one daughter, the husband's brother and sister and the brother's wife and son.

1. Draw a diagram to correspond with the following generalization and description:

(a) *Generalization* A nuclear family may be extended by the addition of both consanguineal and affinal relatives.

(b) *Description*   This nuclear family consists of a husband and wife, the husband's sister and her husband and their son and the son's wife.

2. Write a generalization and a description to correspond with the following diagram:

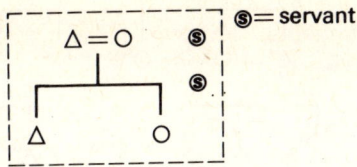

Ⓢ= servant

EXERCISE H *Information transfer: identifying kin*

1. Complete the following table by filling in the terms used in your own language (called here 'L1') for the relatives shown in Column I.

I *Kin formula*	II *English term*	III *Term in L1*
Fa	father	
Mo	mother	
FaFa	grandfather	
MoFa	grandfather	
FaMo	grandmother	
MoMo	grandmother	
FaBr	uncle	
MoBr	uncle	
FaSi	aunt	
MoSi	aunt	
FaBrWi	aunt	
FaSiHu	uncle	

(FaFa=Father's father, MoFa=Mother's father, FaSi=Father's sister, FaBrWi= Father's brother's wife, etc.)

2. Indicate the relationship between ego (⊘ in the diagram overleaf) and the other people who are shown. Use a kin formula and make a statement both in English and in your own language. For example:

Kin formula	*English*	*L1*
C=FaFa	C is ego's grandfather	. . . . . .

$$\triangle^A = O^B$$

$$\triangle^C = O^D \qquad O^E \qquad \triangle^F = O^G$$

$$\triangle^H = O^I \qquad \oslash \qquad \triangle^J \qquad O^K$$

$$\triangle^L \qquad O^M$$

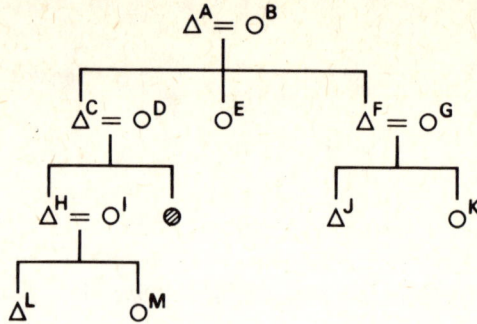

EXERCISE I   *Discourse development*

In Exercises F and G, the descriptions are used to illustrate, or exemplify, the definitions and generalizations.

1. Combine (a) and (b) in each case to make a short passage and show the relationship between (a) and (b) by using the expression FOR EXAMPLE (or FOR INSTANCE). Here is an example from Exercise F:

   A nuclear family is a group consisting of a man and a woman and their offspring sharing a common residence. This, FOR EXAMPLE (FOR IN-STANCE) is a nuclear family consisting of a man and a woman, their two sons and one daughter.

2. Use descriptions to exemplify the definitions and generalizations expressed in the following diagrams:

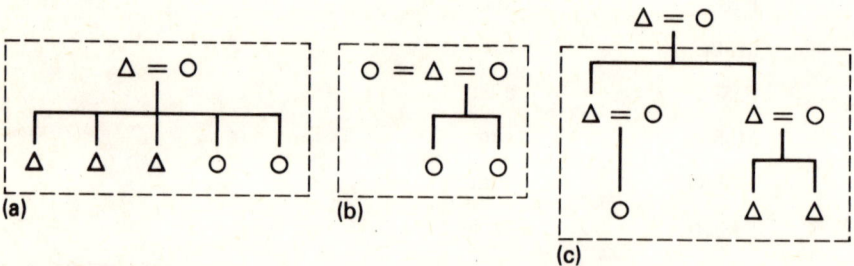

(a) △ = O with offspring △ △ △ O O

(b) O = △ = O with offspring O O

(c) △ = O with △ = O and △ = O; first with O, second with △ △

III   GUIDED WRITING

EXERCISE J

Complete the following sentences by filling the blanks with appropriate prepositions:

1. In many societies distinctions are made (between, across) relatives which in English are grouped together (into, under) the same term.
2. The family exists (near, beyond) the limits of the residential boundary.
3. The extent to which ties of kinship and affinity are recognized varies widely (in, on) different societies.
4. Some societies have terms which refer (to, at) one's mother's brother's wife's father (MoBrWiFa), one's father's mother's sister's son's wife (FaMoSiSoWi), and so on.
5. (Outside, within) many societies, ties of kinship and affinity are recognized by people who (outside, within) Western Europe would not be regarded as relatives at all.
6. (Inside, in) English we have only one term 'grandfather' to refer to FaFa and MoFa.
7. The description of such ties (by, on) reference to the terms which are used to talk (through, about) them is one of the complex tasks that a social anthropologist has to undertake.
8. Relatives are not defined (by, in) terms of common residence.
9. We often find that these relatives are clearly distinguished (on, by) different terms in other languages.

EXERCISE K

Arrange the sentences in Exercise J in an appropriate order by giving the number. Begin with Sentence 8.

EXERCISE L

Form the sentences you have arranged in Exercise K into a paragraph. Join the sentences together to form single statements where appropriate by using *and* and *but*. Relate statements where appropriate by using the following expressions:

thus, for example, furthermore, however

The completed paragraph is a continuation of the reading passage.

IV READING AND NOTE-TAKING

EXERCISE M   *Priming questions*

Read the following passage quickly to get a general idea of its contents. Bear these questions in mind:

1. Who or what are the Nuer?
2. Why are cattle important in their society?

3. What are the difficulties in using the English term *father* in describing the Nuer family?

Relatives, however, are not defined in terms of common residence. The family exists beyond the limits of the residential boundary and in many societies ties of kinship and affinity are recognized by people who in Western Europe would not be regarded as relatives at all. Thus, for example, some societies have terms which refer to one's mother's brother's wife's father (MoBrWiFa), one's father's mother's sister's son's wife (FaMoSiSoWi) and so on. Furthermore, in many societies distinctions are made between relatives which in English-speaking societies are grouped together under the same term. For example, in English we have only one term 'grandfather' to refer to FaFa and MoFa but we often find that these relatives are clearly distinguished by different terms in other languages. The extent to which ties of kinship and affinity are recognized varies widely in different societies and the description of such ties by reference to the terms which are used to talk about them is one of the complex tasks that a social anthropologist has to undertake.

We have spoken of marriage as a formal contract. It should be noted, however, that this contract does not take the same form in different societies. In Western societies, the union of a man and a woman is given the status of legal marriage by being registered by an official recognized by the state. In some African societies, however, marriage has nothing to do with an official registration of this kind but is legalized by the formal exchange of goods. Generally it is the bridegroom who is required to make a payment of goods to the bride's kin, though sometimes a payment is also made by the bridegroom's kin to that of the bride.

Among the Nuer, a people living in Southern Sudan, the payment made to the bride's kin, known as bridewealth, is in the form of cattle. Once the amount of bridewealth is agreed upon, and the formal payment is made, the marriage becomes a legal union and the offspring of the union become the legitimate children of the husband. They remain his children even if the wife subsequently leaves him to live with another man. Furthermore, the giving and receiving of bridewealth represents so binding a contract that even if the wife has children by the man with whom she lives after leaving her husband, these children will be legally her husband's, so long as the cattle offered at the time of the marriage remain the property of the wife's kin. The male offspring from the second and illegal union of the woman will inherit not from his real father but from the woman's husband, and the bridewealth given for the female offspring of this second union at the time of their marriage will go not to their real father but to their mother's legal husband. Thus a distinction has to be made between a natural father, or genitor, and a legal father, or pater, and between natural and legal children.

Once a marriage has been made legal by the giving and receiving of bridewealth then it remains a permanent union and cannot be dissolved. Even the death of the husband does not cause dissolution of the marriage. Among the Nuer, a man's heir is his older brother, who not only inherits his possessions but also takes on the domestic responsibilities of his dead brother. This means that he becomes the guardian of his brother's widow, or widows, and of his children. If a widow is still young he may live with her as a substitute for her husband, but the children that are born from this union will not be his but his dead brother's. Only when bridewealth is returned can a marriage be dissolved.

EXERCISE N *Notes*

Now read the passage more slowly and carefully and complete the following notes:

Paragraph 2

marriage – formal contract.
In Western societies registered
by state official. In some
African societies by . . .
Examples of this . . .

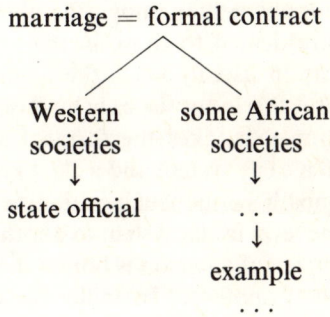

marriage = formal contract

Western societies → state official

some African societies → . . . → example . . .

Paragraph 3

Among Nuer – father
may be pater if . . .
exchanged and then his
offspring are . . .
Father is . . . if no
bridewealth has been
exchanged and his
offspring not legal but
only natural children.

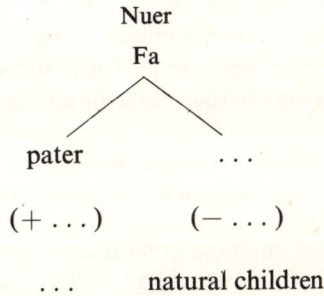

Nuer
Fa

pater (+ . . .) . . .

(− . . .) natural children

DISCUSSION

What aspects of kinship in your own society do you think would need to be explained to a foreigner?

2 Social stratification

---

[1]If we look at the structure of societies, it will be seen that they are divided into different levels, or strata. [2]A society is stratified in the sense that different sections of the community are differentiated according to the amount of income or power they enjoy. [3]People in the higher social levels have privileges which are denied to those in the lower strata. [4]In Western societies, this stratification usually takes the form of differentiation according to social class. [5]But this is not the only kind of social stratification. [6]In some societies, for example, it takes the form of a caste system. [7]One major difference between a caste system and a class system is that in the former an individual is assigned a permanent position in his society at birth and cannot move from one level in the system to another, whereas in the latter he can, at least in principle. [8]If a person is born a member of one caste, he cannot become a member of another. [9]In India, for example, a man who is born into the Kshatriya caste cannot move into a higher caste and become a Brahman. nor into a lower caste and become a Vaishya. [10]In a class system, on the other hand, there is a degree of social mobility. [11]If a person is born into one class, he is not bound to remain in it but may, if he has the opportunity, move into another. [12]Thus, someone who is born into a working-class family may in the course of his life become a member of the middle class.

(a) *People at different social levels are differentiated according to wealth.*
(b) *In a caste system there is no social mobility.*

[13]Although the general notion of social class is an easy one to understand, however, it is not easy to define or apply. [14]In Britain, for example, a division is very often made between the working class and the middle class, but if we examine the criteria for making such a distinction, we will find that they are not always very satisfactory. [15]At first sight, it might seem that income is the best indicator of social class. [16]We might choose a certain figure as an annual income, for example £4000, and say that anyone who earns less than this is a member of the working class, whereas anyone earning more belongs to the middle class. [17]However, income is, in fact, not a very reliable guide. [18]In certain occupations which we would normally think of as middle class,

earnings are less than £4000. [19]On the other hand, there are occupations which are normally associated with the working class where people earn more than this sum. [20]A curate and a schoolteacher, for example, who would generally be considered as members of the middle class, may earn less than this figure, and many coalminers and dockers, who would usually be regarded as belonging to the working class, may earn more.

(c) *Income is a reliable indicator of social class.*
(d) *Schoolteaching would normally be considered as a working-class occupation.*

[21]It might seem, then, that occupation is more reliable than income as a criterion of social class, and indeed in a recent survey most of the people who were questioned defined class difference in terms of occupation. [22]There was general agreement that unskilled manual workers, like labourers and street-sweepers, belonged to the working class. [23]It was also generally agreed that people in professional and managerial occupations, like lawyers and business executives, were members of the middle class. [24]However, there was some difference of opinion about where the line between middle and working class occupations should be drawn. [25]Certain groups of manual workers who were questioned during the survey considered themselves as belonging to the middle class. [26]Others thought that they were members of the working class, but included clerical workers as members of this class as well, whereas the majority of the clerical workers in the survey thought of themselves as middle class.

SOLUTIONS

Complete the following statements by referring to the sentences of the passage which are indicated in brackets. Note that sometimes more than one word is required.

(a) People at different . . . (3) have different amounts of wealth or power.
    People at different social levels are . . . (2) according to the amount of wealth or power they have.
i.e. Different . . . (2) are differentiated according to the . . . (3) they have.
= People at different social levels are differentiated according to *the privileges they have.*

(b) In a . . . (6) system an individual cannot move from one level to another.
    In a caste system there is no movement from one . . . (7) to another.

i.e.   In a caste system there is no . . . (10).
    In a caste system there is no social mobility.

(c) It might seem that income is the best . . . (17) to social class. But income is, in fact, not a reliable . . . (15).
=   Income is *not* a reliable indicator of social class.

(d) People in certain . . . (18) which would normally be . . . (19) with the middle class have a lower . . . (16) than people in certain occupations which we normally . . . (18) as lower class . . . (19). We would normally . . . (18) schoolteachers as members of . . . (20).
=   *Schoolteaching would normally be considered a middle-class occupation.*

EXERCISE A   *Meaning assessment*

Refer to the passage and

(a) decide whether the following statements are true or false according to the passage.
(b) write out the true statement which expresses the most central idea.

Paragraph 1
1. Social stratification takes the form of a caste system.
2. Social stratification sometimes takes the form of a class system.
3. Examples of different forms of social stratification are caste systems and class systems.
4. Class systems are common in Western societies.

Paragraph 2
1. Schoolteachers earn less than coalminers.
2. Income is not a reliable indicator of social class.
3. Coalmining would usually be regarded as a middle-class occupation.
4. Dockers and coalminers earn more than schoolteachers.

Paragraph 3
1. Occupation is a reliable indicator of social class.
2. A recent survey showed that manual workers considered themselves members of the middle class.
3. Some clerical workers in the survey thought that they were members of the middle class.
4. Social class cannot be decided only by reference to occupation.

EXERCISE B *Contextual reference*

Refer to the relevant contexts in the reading passage and replace or expand the expressions printed in italics with expressions which make the meaning clear.

1. But *this* is not the only kind of social stratification. (5)
2. In some societies, for example, *it* takes the form of a caste system. (6)
3. One major difference between a caste system and a class system is that in *the former* an individual cannot move from one level in the system to *another*, whereas in *the latter* he can. (7)
4. If a person is born into one class, he is not bound to remain in *it* but may move into *another*. (11)
5. Although the notion of social class is an easy *one* to understand, however, *it* is not easy to define or to apply. (13)
6. In Britain, for example, a division is very often made between the working class and the middle class, but if we examine the criteria for making *such a distinction*, we will find that *they* are not always very satisfactory. (14)
7. We might choose a certain figure as an annual income, for example £4000, and say that anyone who earns less than *this* is a member of the working class. (16)
8. On the other hand, there are occupations which are normally associated with the working class where people earn more than *this sum*. (19)
9. A curate and a schoolteacher may earn less than *this figure*. (20)
10. *Others* thought that they were members of the working class, but included clerical workers as members of this class as well. (26)

EXERCISE C *Summary*

Arrange the final statements in the Solutions and put them together with the following statements to make a summary of the reading passage. Note: the statements are not given in the right order.

1. The way a society is divided into different social levels is called social stratification.
2. Examples of different forms of social stratification are caste systems and class systems.
3. The general idea of social class is easy to understand.
4. In a class system, on the other hand, an individual can, if he has the opportunity, move from one social level to another.
5. But coalminers may earn more than schoolteachers.

6. Occupation is not a reliable guide to social class either.
7. It is not always easy, however, to make a distinction between different social classes.
8. Coalmining, for example, would normally be considered as a working-class occupation.
9. A recent survey showed, for example, that there was no general agreement among manual workers and clerical workers about the classes they belonged to.

II   USE OF LANGUAGE

EXERCISE D   *Contrast within statements*

Consider the following statements:

   (i) In Western societies, social stratification usually takes the form of a class system.
  (ii) In some Asian societies, social stratification takes the form of a caste system.

There are two contrasts here:

  In Western societies/In some Asian societies
  class system/caste system

Where there are two contrasts we can combine the two statements into one contrasting statement by using WHEREAS:

  (iii) In Western societies, social differentiation usually takes the form of a class system, WHEREAS in some Asian societies it (i.e. social differentiation) takes the form of a caste system.

    or

  (iv) In some Asian societies, social differentiation takes the form of a caste system, WHEREAS in Western societies it usually takes the form of a class system.

    or

  (v) WHEREAS in Western societies social differentiation takes the form of a class system, in some Asian societies it takes the form of a caste system.

    or

  (vi) WHEREAS . . . (Write out this contrasting statement.)

Select pairs of generalizations from the following set which can be contrasted, write down the contrasts (see above) and then combine the pairs of generalizations into contrasting statements.

1. Consanguineal relatives are related by birth.
2. A polygynous family includes one husband and more than one wife.
3. In a caste system there is no social mobility.
4. Affinal relatives are related by marriage.
5. In a polygamous family there are more than two spouses.
6. In a caste system a person cannot move from one social level to another.
7. Lawyers are considered to be members of the middle class.
8. In a monogamous family there are only two spouses.
9. There is social mobility in a class system.
10. Labourers are considered to be members of the working class.
11. A polyandrous family includes one wife and more than one husband.
12. In a class system a person can, in principle, move from one social level to another.

EXERCISE E   *Contrast between statements*

If there are two ideas in contrast, WHEREAS can be used to combine two single statements into one contrasting statement. We can use ON THE OTHER HAND to show that one statement contrasts with another statement. WHEREAS *combines* two statements to make one contrasting statement. ON THE OTHER HAND *relates* two statements to show that they are in contrast. For example:

> In Western societies, social differentiation usually takes the form of a class system, WHEREAS in some Asian societies it takes the form of a caste system.

= In Western societies, social differentiation usually takes the form of a class system. . . . In some Asian societies, ON THE OTHER HAND, social differentiation takes the form of a caste system.

If the first idea in the second statement is a contrasting idea, ON THE OTHER HAND usually comes after it. If the first idea is not a contrasting idea, ON THE OTHER HAND usually comes before it.

> *In Western societies*, social differentiation usually takes the form of a class system. . . . *In some Asian societies*, ON THE OTHER HAND, social differentiation takes the form of a caste system.

In some Asian societies is the first idea in the second statement and it contrasts with *In Western societies* in the first statement.

> Social differentiation usually takes the form of a class system in Western societies. . . . ON THE OTHER HAND, social differentiation takes the form of a caste system in some Asian societies.

not

> Social differentiation usually takes the form of a class system in Western societies. . . . Social differentiation, ON THE OTHER HAND, takes the form of a caste system in some Asian societies.

Social differentiation is the first idea in the second statement and it is not in contrast with any idea in the first statement – it is an idea that both statements have in common.

Now use ON THE OTHER HAND to relate the pairs of statements in Exercise D above.

EXERCISE F   *Information transfer: statements of contrast*

1. Read the following account of earnings in Ruritania and complete the table below.

In 1950, the average earnings of an accountant were approximately $5000, whereas farmworkers were earning, on average, only about $2000. Bus drivers were slightly better off at about $2500, but even this was hardly an adequate wage. As time went by, the situation became worse. By 1965, accountants had doubled their salary and so had bus drivers. Farm-workers, on the other hand, had not kept up with these increases. Their annual wages were approximately $3500, which was what schoolteachers were earning 15 years before! Five years later, the earnings of bus drivers had risen to $7000 and accountants were now getting three times as much as in 1950. The farmworkers, on the other hand, had fallen even further behind. The increase of $500 they got in 1970 was in fact smaller than the increase in the cost of living. So in 1970, farmworkers were in effect earning less than in 1965, whereas accountants, schoolteachers, and indeed all non-manual workers, were earning a good deal more.

TABLE   *Approximate earnings in Ruritania ($)*

Occupation	1950	1955	1960	1965	1970
Accountant		6500	7500		
Doctor	4500	5500	7500	8000	9500
Schoolteacher		4000	5500	6000	7000
Bus driver	2500	3000	3500		
Farmworker		2500	2500		

2. Draw a completed version of the following graph so that it accounts for all the information contained in the table.

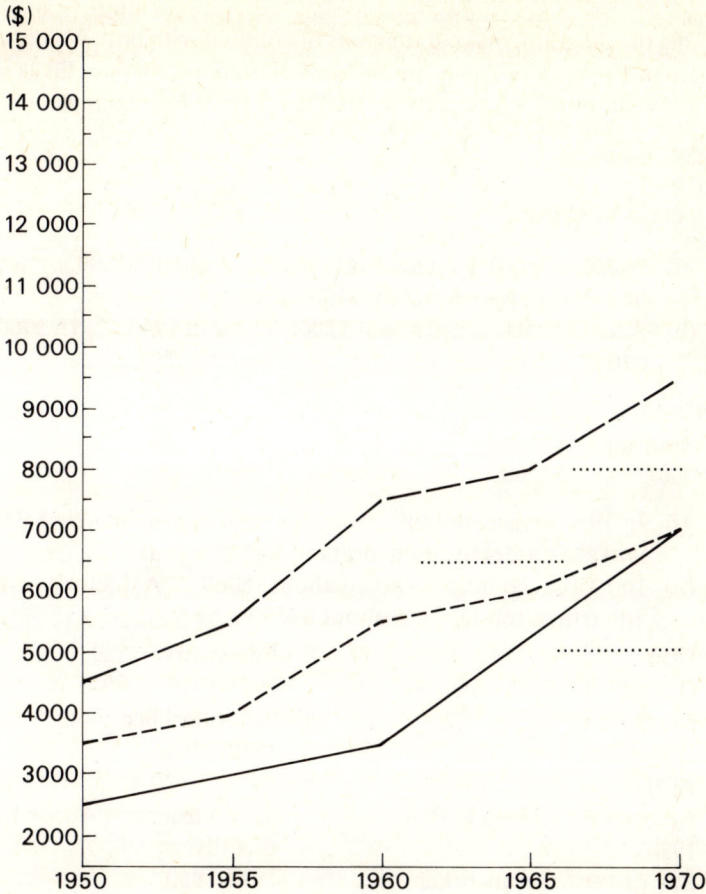

3. The following diagram shows alternative ways of saying the same thing.

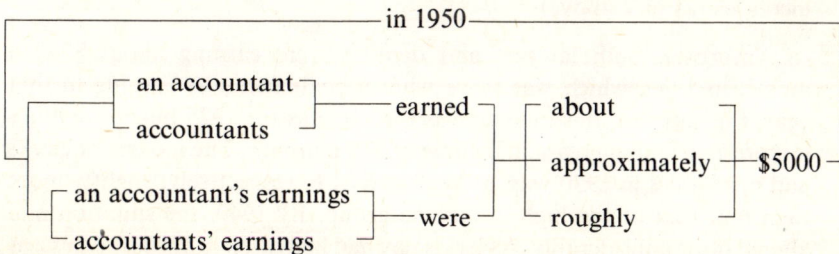

For example:

In 1950 an accountant earned roughly $5000.
= An accountant's earnings were about $5000 in 1950.

Using the diagram, make statements of contrast with both WHEREAS and ON THE OTHER HAND by reference to the table of earnings on page 20 as indicated below. Write out the contrasts in note form first. For example:

Accountant
1950   1960
$5000 $7500

  (i)   WHEREAS in 1950 an accountant earned about $5000 a year, in 1960 he earned approximately $7500 a year.
 (ii) Accountants earned about $5000 a year in 1950 . . . In 1960, ON THE OTHER HAND, their earnings were about $7500 a year.

1950
Accountant   Doctor
$5000 $4500

  (i)   In 1950 an accountant's earnings were approximately $5000 a year WHEREAS a doctor earned about $4500 a year.
 (ii) In 1950, accountants earned about $5000 . . . A doctor's earnings, ON THE OTHER HAND, were about $4500 a year.

(a) 1950
    Doctor   Farmworker
(b) Accountant
    1955 1970
(c) 1970
    Accountant   Farmworker
(d) 1950
    Bus driver   Farmworker
(e) Doctor
    1950 1970

(f) Farmworker
    1965 1970
(g) Schoolteacher
    1950 1965
(h) 1955
    Schoolteacher   Accountant
(i) Bus driver
    1970 1950
(j) 1960
    Doctor   Bus driver

4. Read the following account of earnings in Ambrosia and draw up a table of approximate incomes (as in 1 above) and a graph showing the relative increases (as in 2 above).

In Ambrosia, both lawyers and dentists were earning about $240 a month in 1930, which was twice what a coalminer was earning in that year. For lawyers, this income was the same as for 1925 but for dentists it represented an increase in income of $30 a month. The income of clerks and mechanics in 1930 was, at $130 and $140 respectively, slightly more than half that of the highest income group. By 1940, the situation had altered quite considerably. A clerk's pay had increased to $200 (the same as a dentist's earnings twenty years before) and a mechanic's to $220 whereas coalminers were now earning double wha' they had earned in 1930 and three times their income of 1920 and 1925. By 1945 a coalminer's pay had increased to around $320; these earnings were $20 a month more than those of mechanics, $100 a month more than those of clerks and only $90 a month less than those of dentists and $140 less than those of lawyers. So in 1945, the income of clerks and lawyers had doubled since 1920, that of mechanics had trebled and that of coalminers had increased four times. It is interesting to note that whereas in 1925 the highest income (that of lawyers) was four times greater than the lowest (that of miners), by 1945 the highest income (still that of lawyers) was only just over twice as great as the lowest. The lowest income now, however, was that of the clerks.

EXERCISE G *Discourse development*

The general statement

(i) in Western societies, social stratification takes the form of a class system

can be expanded. The *expansion* takes the form of a less general statement which counts as an *example*:

(ii) In Britain, FOR EXAMPLE, a distinction is usually made between the middle class and the working class.

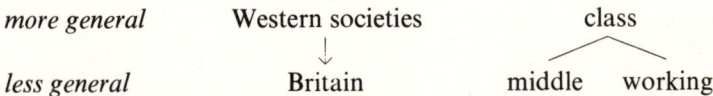

| *more general* | Western societies | class |
| *less general* | Britain | middle working |

A contrasting statement

(iii) in some Asian societies, social stratification takes the form of a caste system

can also have an expansion in the same way:

(iv) In India, FOR EXAMPLE, a distinction is usually made between four main castes: the Brahmans, the Kshatriyas, the Vaishyas and the Sudras.

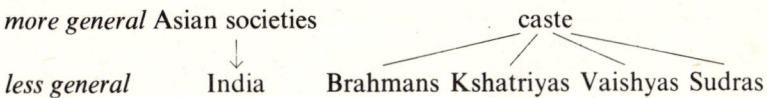

| *more general* Asian societies | caste |
| *less general* India | Brahmans Kshatriyas Vaishyas Sudras |

When (i) and (iii) are combined to form a single contrastive statement, it is the second part which can be expanded by an example:

(i), WHEREAS (iii)+(iv)

In Western societies, social stratification takes the form of a class system, WHEREAS in some Asian societies, it takes the form of a caste system. In India, FOR EXAMPLE, a distinction is usually made between four main castes: the Brahmans, the Kshatriyas, the Vaishyas and the Sudras.

WHEREAS (i), (iii)+(iv)

WHEREAS in Western societies social stratification takes the form of a class system, in some Asian societies, it takes the form of a caste system. In India, FOR EXAMPLE, a distinction . . . etc.

Now write out passages for the following:

(iii), WHEREAS (i)+(ii)
WHEREAS (iii), (i)+(ii)

When (i) and (iii) are related to form two contrasting statements, the first statement can be expanded:

$$(i)+(ii)+\left\{\begin{matrix} \text{ON THE OTHER HAND} \\ \text{(iii)} \end{matrix}\right\}$$

In Western societies, social stratification takes the form of a class system. In Britain, FOR EXAMPLE, a distinction is usually made between the middle class and the working class. In some Asian societies, ON THE OTHER HAND, social stratification takes the form of a caste system.

$$(iii)+(iv)+\left\{\begin{matrix} \text{ON THE OTHER HAND} \\ \text{(i)} \end{matrix}\right\}$$

In some Asian societies, social stratification takes the form of a caste system. In India, FOR EXAMPLE, a distinction is usually made between four main castes: the Brahmans, the Kshatriyas, the Vaishyas and the Sudras. In Western societies, ON THE OTHER HAND, social stratification takes the form of a class system.

Now link the following groups of statements together, *where possible*, by using WHEREAS, ON THE OTHER HAND, and FOR EXAMPLE.

1. (a) In a class system there is social mobility.
   (b) In a caste system an individual cannot move from one social level to another.
   (c) A member of the working class may, if he has the opportunity, become middle class in the course of his life.
2. (a) Some people who would be regarded as middle class earn less than some people who would be regarded as working class.
   (b) A schoolteacher sometimes earns less than an electrician.
   (c) A coalminer sometimes earns more than a bank clerk.
3. (a) Brothers-in-law and sisters-in-law are affinal relatives.
   (b) Consanguineal relatives are people who are related by birth.
   (c) Affinal relatives are related by marriage.

4. (a) There is only one wife and one husband in a monogamous family.
   (b) In a polyandrous family there is more than one husband and in a polygynous family there is more than one wife.
   (c) In a polygamous family there are more than two spouses.
5. (a) Individuals can in principle move from one class to another.
   (b) There is no movement of individuals from one caste to another.
   (c) Someone who is born a Brahman or a Vaishya remains a member of that caste.
6. (a) In some societies, servants live as members of the family they work for.
   (b) Sometimes a family is extended by the addition of non-relatives.
   (c) Sometimes families are extended by the addition of the wife's kin.
7. (a) Many workers in West Germany come from Yugoslavia and Turkey.
   (b) A family may be incomplete because of economic necessity.
   (c) Sometimes a man has to leave his family to work in another country.
8. (a) A nuclear family is generally established by marriage.
   (b) In Western Europe the couple in a nuclear family are usually legally married as husband and wife.
9. (a) In some societies a family is incomplete because of convention.
   (b) There are societies where the family is incomplete by reason of economic necessity.
   (c) Sometimes a man has to leave his family to find work in another part of the country or in a different country altogether.

III   GUIDED WRITING

EXERCISE H

Arrange the words in brackets in such a way as to compose correct sentences. For example:

The fact that the occupation of manual workers (of was prestige lower partly because of was) the lower income of manual workers.
The fact that the occupation of manual workers *was of lower prestige was partly because of* the lower income of manual workers.

1. The fact that the occupation of manual workers (was of also because partly prestige lower) the clerical workers generally had a better education.
2. A general increase in educational opportunity (that meant has) clerical occupations (more now are available widely) to the children of manual workers.
3. The occupation of manual workers (of lower was prestige).

4. (thirty past the so or over years), the income of many manual workers has risen above the income of the majority of clerical workers.
5. In the past, manual workers (if they even skilled were), usually earned less than people in clerical occupations.
6. A difficulty in using occupation as a criterion of class (of absence the general is agreement) among the population as to which occupations are associated with which classes.
7. The difficulty in using occupation (as criterion of a class) is (evident particularly in) the assessment of clerical occupations.
8. The prestige of clerical occupations (considerably in has years fallen recent).

EXERCISE I

Arrange the sentences in Exercise H into an appropriate order. When this is done some phrases can be replaced with pronouns. Find those phrases in the sentences indicated below and replace them with the pronouns suggested.

8 this   4 their   1 this   2 it   5 that

EXERCISE J

Form the sentences you have arranged in Exercise I into a paragraph by: (a) joining sentences to make single statements where appropriate by using the following expressions: *and*, *but*; and (b) relating statements where appropriate by using the following expressions: *then*, *however*, *in consequence*, *furthermore*. The completed paragraph is a continuation of the reading passage in Section I above.

IV   READING AND NOTE-TAKING

EXERCISE K   *Priming questions*

Read the following passage quickly to get a general idea of its contents. Bear these questions in mind:

1. How far are castes associated with particular occupations?
2. What is the difference between a caste system and an age-grade system?

A difficulty in using occupation as a criterion of class, then, is the absence of general agreement among the population as to which occupations are associated with which classes. This is particularly evident in the assessment of clerical occupations. In the past, manual workers, even if they were skilled, usually earned less than people in clerical occupations and their occupations were of lower prestige. This was partly because of their lower income but it was also partly because clerical workers were better educated. Over the past thirty years or so, however, the income of many manual workers has risen above that of the majority of clerical workers. Furthermore, a general increase in educational opportunity has meant that clerical occupations are now more widely available to the children of manual workers. In consequence, the prestige of clerical occupations has fallen considerably in recent years.

There is of course no difficulty about deciding what caste a person belongs to because he is assigned to a particular caste at birth and remains a member of that caste for the rest of his life. It would seem that in this respect social stratification which takes the form of a caste system is simpler than that which takes the form of a class system. There are, however, certain complicating factors. If we look at the caste system in India, for example, it will be seen that it operates at two distinct levels.

At one level, there is a general classification of people into castes which applies throughout the whole country. These castes are known as *varna*. There are four of these and the whole Hindu population of India is divided into members of one or the other of them. The highest of these castes is that of the Brahmans or priests. The next highest is the varna of the warriors, known as the Kshatriya, or sometimes as the Rajput caste. Below this comes the Vaishya or merchant caste and the lowest caste is known as the Sudra caste. It will be noticed that castes are traditionally associated with a type of occupation. But in modern India, of course, members of the Brahman caste are not all priests and members of the Kshatriya caste are not all warriors and occupations are no longer a reliable guide to caste.

Although we can describe the caste system in India in general in terms of these four different varna, however, caste operates rather differently at the more particular level of village life. In Indian villages, caste generally takes the form of a division of the community into different social groups called *jati*. The members of these local castes tend to have the same occupation and they maintain caste divisions by forbidding marriage between members of different jati. As with the varna, these village castes are differentiated according to status so that one jati is higher in prestige than another. That is to say, they form a hierarchy of different degrees of superiority. Whereas, as we have seen, occupation is not a reliable guide to social class nor to the general varna caste system, it is a reasonably good guide to caste at the village level because particular jati do tend to be associated with particular occupations.

Although class and caste are the two best known forms of social stratification, they are not the only ones. In parts of Africa and among the Aborigines of Australia, for example, there are societies which are differentiated according to age-grades. As the boys in these societies grow up, they move from one definite age-grade to another, from boy to unmarried youth to married adult and so on. Each age-grade is associated with a particular occupation so that in the course of his life the individual becomes a hunter, a warrior and finally, in the last age-grade, an elder of the community. In societies like these, then, society is stratified according to age. As we have seen, in a caste system an individual remains in the social stratum in which he is born, whereas in an age-grade system the individual moves from one stratum to another automatically as he gets older. In this respect, there is social mobility in an age-grade system, whereas there is no such social mobility in a caste system. On the other hand, the mobility in an age-grade system is of course not the same as that which we find in a class system.

EXERCISE L   *Notes*

Now read the passage more slowly and carefully and complete the following notes.

Paragraph 2
caste system
general level = varna
local (e.g. village) level = . . .
varna high → . . .
Brahman, Kshatriya (or . . .), . . . and . . .

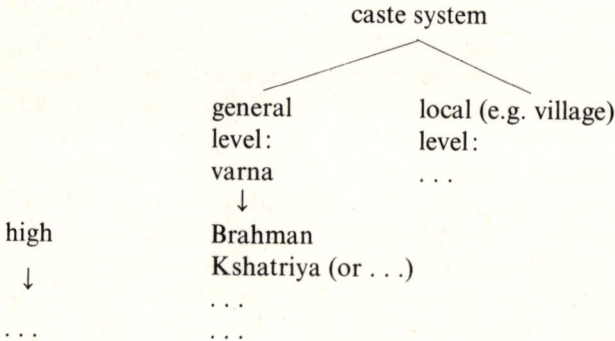

caste system

	general level: varna ↓	local (e.g. village) level: . . .
high ↓	Brahman Kshatriya (or . . .) . . .	
. . .	. . .	

Paragraph 3
social stratification
three kinds: class, . . . (e.g. India) and . . . (e.g. Aborigines).
Degrees of social mobility in kinds of social stratification from high to low: . . . , . . . and . . . , which is the lowest.

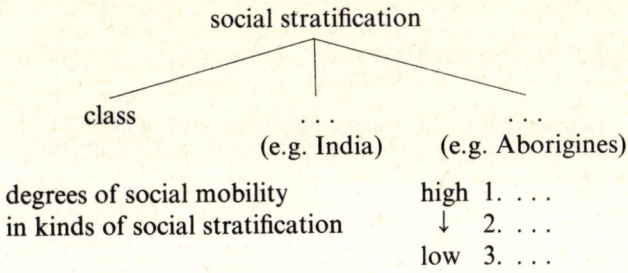

```
                    social stratification
                 ┌─────────────┼─────────────┐
        class              . . .           . . .
                        (e.g. India)    (e.g. Aborigines)
  degrees of social mobility        high  1. . . .
  in kinds of social stratification   ↓   2. . . .
                                     low   3. . . .
```

DISCUSSION

What kind of social stratification do you have in your own country? How does it affect social mobility?

3 Social learning

---

[1]As a child grows up, he learns how to behave in ways which are appropriate to the society into which he is born. [2]That is to say, he acquires the patterns of behaviour which are accepted as normal in his society. [3]This process of social learning is generally referred to as socialization. [4]By socialization, then, we mean the process whereby individuals learn the rules, values and practices of the society in which they live. [5]Generally speaking, we can say that this is brought about in two ways: firstly, as a result of the child's upbringing, or the natural interaction with the members of his family and other people in his immediate social environment, and, secondly, as a result of formal education. [6]In some societies we find a certain degree of formal instruction included as part of the upbringing of the child. [7]This occurs, for example, when children are taught certain kinds of ritual behaviour by members of their family or local community. [8]In most societies, however, formal education is differentiated from upbringing and is conducted as a separate operation. [9]Although this is an over-simplification, let us for the moment use the term 'primary socialization' to refer to social learning that takes place as part of upbringing, as a consequence of the individual's participation in the life of his family and his immediate community. [10]The social learning that results from formal education we will refer to as 'secondary socialization'.

(a) *Socialization refers to the way an individual acquires appropriate social behaviour.*

(b) *Social learning which occurs through upbringing can be referred to as secondary socialization.*

[11]It is possible to argue that the differentiation of the two kinds of socialization is to some extent explained by reference to the complex manpower requirements of the modern state. [12]The social learning acquired through upbringing often needs to be extended because it does not provide for the national need in many countries for trained personnel like clerical workers, technicians, civil servants and so on. [13]In this respect secondary socialization can be regarded as complementary to primary socialization. [14]The former, we might say, provides the individual with skills which allow him to take on

specialist employment and to have a role in a larger social environment, whereas the latter allows him to be integrated into the particular social group into which he is born. [15]Thus we might argue that primary socialization defines the individual's role in a small social group and enables him to identify himself as a member of his family and his local community. [16]Secondary socialization, on the other hand, provides for the individual's role in society as a whole and enables him to identify himself as a citizen of the state. [17]In short, and to oversimplify, we might say that the first kind of socialization provides a sense of security and social integration whereas the second provides opportunity and the possibility of social mobility.

(c) *Secondary socialization provides for the specialist manpower needs of the modern state.*
(d) *Primary socialization allows the individual to be an integrated member of his immediate community.*

[18]However, although it can be argued that the two forms of socialization support each other, it is also true that in some respects they may be in conflict. [19]The ways of thinking which are taught in formal education are often contrary to those learned in primary socialization. [20]Indeed, it is often the very purpose of education to replace patterns of thought and behaviour which have been acquired through primary socialization with others which are considered to be more rational or efficient. [21]For example, there may be certain ritualistic or religious practices which are based on beliefs which are contrary to scientific fact. [22]Again, certain social customs may be inconsistent with principles of efficiency in production and management. [23]The way in which a language is used in formal education, and in some cases the actual language itself, may be very different from what the learner is accustomed to in the social environment of his home and local community. [24]As he learns new ways of using language, the patterns of thinking acquired in primary socialization will tend to be changed.

SOLUTIONS

Complete the following statements by referring to the sentences of the passage which are indicated in brackets. Note that sometimes more than one word is required.

(a) As a child grows up, he learns the . . . (2) which are accepted as normal in his society.
=   The child learns behaviour which is . . . (1) to his society.
i.e. The child learns appropriate . . . (3) behaviour.
i.e. The individual . . . (2) appropriate social behaviour.
      The way an individual acquires appropriate social behaviour is referred to as . . . (3).

=   *Socialization refers to the way an individual acquires appropriate social behaviour.*

(b)   We can use the term 'secondary socialization' to refer to . . . (3) which takes place in . . . (5).

i.e.   The term 'secondary socialization' refers here to social learning which . . . (7) through formal education.

=   Social learning which occurs through *formal education* can be referred to as secondary socialization.

(c)   . . . (9) does not usually provide for the . . . (11) needs of a modern state. The modern state has . . . (11) for specialist . . . (12).

i.e.   The modern state has specialist . . . (11) needs. . . . (13) can provide for the specialist manpower needs of the modern state.

=   Secondary socialization *can provide* for the specialist manpower needs of the modern state.

(d)   Primary socialization enables the . . . (14) to become a member of his . . . (15) community.
Primary socialization allows the individual to have a sense of . . . (17) with his local community.

i.e.   Primary socialization allows the individual to be an integrated . . . (15) of his . . . (9) community.

=   *Primary socialization allows the individual to be an integrated member of his immediate community.*

EXERCISE A   *Meaning assessment*

Refer to the passage and

(a)   decide whether the following statements are true or false according to the passage.
(b)   write out the true statement which expresses the most central idea.

Paragraph 1
1.   Social learning takes place only by means of formal education.
2.   Certain kinds of ritual behaviour are taught by formal instruction.
3.   The child is socialized both by his upbringing and by his education at school.
4.   Primary socialization takes place at home.

Paragraph 2
1.   Primary socialization does not usually provide specialist training.
2.   Both primary and secondary socialization provide the individual with social identity.
3.   Primary socialization gives the individual an opportunity to move away from his local community.

Paragraph 3
1. Religious belief is contrary to scientific fact.
2. Social customs lead to inefficiency.
3. Primary and secondary socialization may sometimes be in conflict.
4. The child often learns new ways of using language at school.

EXERCISE B   *Contextual reference*

Refer to the relevant contexts in the reading passage and replace or expand the expressions printed in italics with expressions which make the meaning clear.

1. Generally speaking, we can say that *this* is brought about in two ways. (5)
2. *This* occurs when children are taught certain kinds of ritual behaviour. (7)
3. *This* is an oversimplification. (9)
4. *It* does not provide for the national need in many countries for trained personnel. (12)
5. *The former* provides the individual with skills which allow him to take up specialist employment whereas *the latter* allows him to be integrated into the particular social group into which he is born. (14)
6. *The first kind of socialization* provides a sense of security whereas *the second* provides opportunity. (17)
7. The ways of thinking which are taught in formal education are often contrary to *those* learned in primary socialization. (19)
8. It is often the very purpose of education to replace patterns of thought and behaviour which have been acquired through primary socialization with *others* which are considered to be more rational or efficient. (20)

EXERCISE C   *Summary*

Arrange the final statements in the Solutions and put them together with the following statements to make a summary of the reading passage. Note: the statements are not given in the right order.

1. We can refer to the first as primary socialization.
2. For example, the patterns of thought learned through formal education may sometimes contradict those acquired through upbringing.
3. This social learning takes place through upbringing on the one hand and formal education on the other.
4. This is social learning which is a consequence of the child's interaction with his family and local community.
5. The two kinds of social learning can, however, be in conflict.
6. The two forms of socialization can be regarded as complementary.

II   USE OF LANGUAGE

EXERCISE D   *Corrective statements*

Part I

Consider the following statements:

(i) Formal education and upbringing are combined.
(ii) Formal education and upbringing are separate operations.

These statements are contradictions. Either (i) is true or (ii) is true but both cannot be true.

We can add a qualifying expression in each case (see Unit 1, Exercise E) so that these statements are not contradictions:

(iii) Formal education and upbringing are *sometimes* combined.
(iv) Formal education and upbringing are *usually* separate operations.

Both of these statements may be true.

To make clear that these statements are not contradictory, we can combine them into one statement by using ALTHOUGH or BUT:

(v) ALTHOUGH formal education and upbringing are sometimes combined, they are usually separate operations.
(vi) Formal education and upbringing are sometimes combined BUT they are usually separate operations.

The second part of these statements corrects any possible over-generalization from what is said in the first part. We can call them *corrective statements*.

Statement	*Possible over-generalization*	*Corrective statement*
Formal education and upbringing are sometimes combined.	Formal education and upbringing are (always) combined.	Formal education and upbringing are *usually* separate operations (i.e. usually not combined).

Make corrective statements with ALTHOUGH and BUT by combining each statement on the left with the appropriate statement on the right. Write down the possible over-generalization first. For example:

(a) Family life has an important influence on the child.

(b) He learns appropriate behaviour.
(c) The local community also exerts an influence upon him.
(d) He is not influenced by the family.

Possible over-generalization: There is no other influence on the child.

Corrective statements

ALTHOUGH (a), (c)
ALTHOUGH family life has an important influence on the child, the local community also exerts an influence upon him.

(a) BUT (c)
Family life has an important influence on the child BUT the local community also exerts an influence upon him.

Note: (b) does not correct any possible over-generalization and (d) is a contradiction of (a). We cannot have:
ALTHOUGH (a), (b) or (a) BUT (b)
ALTHOUGH (a), (d) or (a) BUT (d)

1. (a) The nuclear family is usually established by a formal contract of marriage.
   (b) It consists of a couple and their offspring.
   (c) It is not always complete.
   (d) It can also be established by concubinage.

2. (a) Families are often incomplete because of economic necessity.
   (b) They are sometimes incomplete because of social convention.
   (c) The man sometimes has to leave the family to work elsewhere.
   (d) Incomplete families are the result of social convention.

3. (a) The nuclear family can be defined as a couple living with their children in the same home.
   (b) Sometimes the couple is not married.
   (c) They do not share the same residence.
   (d) The family may sometimes be incomplete.

4. (a) There are generally two spouses in most families.
   (b) In polygamous families there are more than two.
   (c) Monogamy is a very common form of marriage.
   (d) The family is sometimes extended.

5. (a) In Western societies, social stratification usually takes the form of a class system.
   (b) This system provides for social mobility.
   (c) It takes the form of a caste system.
   (d) This is not the only way in which society is stratified.

6. (a) The notion of social class is a familiar one.
   (b) It is easy to define.
   (c) It is not easy to define.
   (d) The notion of caste is not easy to define.

7. (a) Middle-class people tend to earn more than working-class people.
   (b) Members of the working class earn less than middle-class people.
   (c) They have more prestige.
   (d) Income is not a reliable indicator of social class.

8. (a) Most people agreed that lawyers and accountants were middle-class people.
   (b) There was a difference of opinion about other occupations.
   (c) Most people agreed that coal-miners belonged to the working class.
   (d) Clerical workers thought of themselves as middle class.

9. (a) Primary socialization has an important function.
   (b) It is the result of upbringing.
   (c) It does not always provide for the needs of a modern state.
   (d) Secondary socialization occurs through formal education.

10. (a) Primary and secondary socialization ought to be complementary.
    (b) Primary socialization has an important function.
    (c) They are sometimes in conflict.
    (d) They ought to support each other.

11. (a) Castes are traditionally associated with certain occupations.
    (b) Brahmans were traditionally priests.
    (c) There is no social mobility in a caste system.
    (d) Occupation is no longer a reliable guide to caste.

12. (a) The caste system seems to be a simple one.
    (b) There are complications.
    (c) The class system is more familiar.
    (d) It differs from the class system.

Part II

In corrective statements with ALTHOUGH and BUT, the second part of the statement corrects any possible over-generalization which might arise from the first part.

The second part can also be used as a corrective statement on its own. Then BUT or HOWEVER is used to indicate that the second statement corrects any possible over-generalization that might arise from the first:

Formal education and upbringing are sometimes combined. BUT they (formal education and upbringing) are usually separate operations.

Formal education and upbringing are sometimes combined. They are usually, HOWEVER, separate operations.

ALTHOUGH *combines* two statements to make one corrective statement.
HOWEVER *relates* two statements to show that the second corrects the first.
BUT can be used either to combine or to relate statements.

Note:
BUT always appears at the beginning of the sentence.
HOWEVER may appear, between commas, in a number of positions in the sentence, except that it does not usually appear after the subject if the subject is a pronoun.

Relate the appropriate statements in Part I above by using BUT and HOWEVER. For example:

Family life has an important influence on the child. BUT the local community also exerts an influence upon him.

Family life has an important influence on the child. The local community, HOWEVER, also exerts an influence upon him.

Family life has an important influence on the child. The local community also, HOWEVER, exerts an important influence upon him.

Family life has an important influence on the child. HOWEVER, the local community also exerts an influence upon him.

EXERCISE E *Discourse development*

Part I

The general statement:

    (i) Formal education and upbringing are sometimes combined.

can be expanded. This *expansion* may take the form of a less general statement which counts as an *example* (see Unit 2, Exercise G).

    (ii) In some societies, FOR EXAMPLE, children are given lessons in ritual by their parents.

The expansion may also take the form of a *clarification*:

    (iii) THAT IS TO SAY, children are given courses of instruction by members of their family or local community.

The expansion may consist of *clarification + example*:

    (iv) (Formal education and upbringing are sometimes combined.) THAT IS TO SAY, children are given courses of instruction by members of their family or local community. In some societies, FOR EXAMPLE, children are given lessons in ritual by their parents.

The corrective statement:

(v)   Formal education and upbringing are usually separate operations

can also be expanded in the same way:

Example
(vi)   In Western Europe, FOR EXAMPLE, parents do not usually teach their children science and teachers do not teach table manners.

Clarification
(vii)   THAT IS TO SAY, what is taught at home is usually quite different from what it taught at school.

Clarification + example
(viii) (Formal education and upbringing are usually separate operations.) THAT IS TO SAY, what is taught at home is usually quite different from what is taught at school. In Western Europe, FOR EXAMPLE, parents do not usually teach their children science and teachers do not teach table manners.

(a)   Practice making corrective statements and expansions by using the formulae given below.

When (i) and (v) are combined to form a single corrective statement, it is the second part that is expanded:

ALTHOUGH (i) (v)+(vi)	(i) BUT (v)+(vi)
ALTHOUGH (i) (v)+(vii)	(i) BUT (v)+(vii)
ALTHOUGH (i) (v)+(viii)	(i) BUT (v)+(viii)
ALTHOUGH (v) (i)+(ii)	(v) BUT (i)+(ii)
ALTHOUGH (v) (i)+(iii)	(v) BUT (i)+(iii)
ALTHOUGH (v) (i)+(iv)	(v) BUT (i)+(iv)

(b)   Expand the statements you have made in Exercise D, Part I above by using appropriate statements from the following with either THAT IS TO SAY or FOR EXAMPLE. (Note that in 3 and 10 both clarification and example are required.) For example:

The couple who live together need not be married.
ALTHOUGH the nuclear family is usually established by a formal contract of marriage, it can also be established by concubinage. THAT IS TO SAY, the couple who live together need not be married.

1. A person in a 'middle class' occupation, like a curate, often earns less than someone in a 'working class' occupation, like a miner.
2. Some people thought that clerical workers were middle class whereas others thought that they were members of the working class.
3. (a) Either the man or the woman may be absent from the home.
   (b) It may be necessary for the man to find work in another part of the country.
4. Formal education often introduces ideas and attitudes which are contrary to those acquired through upbringing.
5. In societies where polygyny is practised, there is more than one wife, and in societies where polyandry is practised, there is more than one husband.
6. Among the Ashanti, a man and his wife live with their own kin after marriage.
7. Vaishyas were traditionally merchants but many people of that caste are not merchants nowadays and many merchants do not belong to the Vaishya caste.
8. The caste system which operates at village level, or *jati*, is not the same as that which operates at a more general level, which is known as *varna*.
9. In some societies, social stratification takes the form of a caste system.
10. (a) It does not meet the requirement for trained personnel of society as a whole.
    (b) An engineer and a doctor have to be given special training through formal education.
11. It is not easy to provide accurate criteria for deciding whether someone belongs to one class or another.

Part II

When there is an expansion between a statement and a corrective statement with HOWEVER or BUT, the first statement is usually repeated and combined with the second statement with ALTHOUGH.

$$(\text{i}) + (\text{ii}) + \text{ALTHOUGH} \left\{ \begin{array}{c} \text{HOWEVER} \\ (\text{i})\ (\text{v}) \end{array} \right\} \qquad (\text{i}) + (\text{ii}) + \text{BUT ALTHOUGH} \ (\text{i})\ (\text{v})$$

e.g. Formal education and upbringing are sometimes combined. In some societies, FOR EXAMPLE, children are given lessons in ritual by their parents. . . . (further expansion) . . . ALTHOUGH formal education and upbringing are sometimes combined, HOWEVER, they are usually separate operations.

Formal education and upbringing are sometimes combined. In some societies, FOR EXAMPLE, children are given lessons in ritual by their parents. . . . BUT ALTHOUGH formal education and upbringing are sometimes combined, they are usually separate operations.

Note: Often, the idea of the first statement is repeated by using a different sentence which means the same thing:

Formal education and upbringing are sometimes combined. In some societies, FOR EXAMPLE, children are given lessons in ritual by their parents. . . . ALTHOUGH education and upbringing sometimes go together, HOWEVER, they are usually separate operations.

(a) Practise making expansions by using the following formulas:

$$(i) + \ (ii) + \text{ALTHOUGH} \left\{ \begin{array}{c} \text{HOWEVER} \\ \text{(i) (v)} \end{array} \right\} \qquad (i) + \ (ii) + \text{BUT ALTHOUGH (i) (v)}$$

$$(i) + \ (iii) + \text{ALTHOUGH} \left\{ \begin{array}{c} \text{HOWEVER} \\ \text{(i) (v)} \end{array} \right\} \qquad (i) + \ (iii) + \text{BUT ALTHOUGH (i) (v)}$$

$$(i) + \ (iv) + \text{ALTHOUGH} \left\{ \begin{array}{c} \text{HOWEVER} \\ \text{(i) (v)} \end{array} \right\} \qquad (i) + \ (iv) + \text{BUT ALTHOUGH (i) (v)}$$

$$(v) + \ (vi) + \text{ALTHOUGH} \left\{ \begin{array}{c} \text{HOWEVER} \\ \text{(v) (i)} \end{array} \right\} \qquad (v) + \ (vi) + \text{BUT ALTHOUGH (v) (i)}$$

$$(v) + \ (vii) + \text{ALTHOUGH} \left\{ \begin{array}{c} \text{HOWEVER} \\ \text{(v) (i)} \end{array} \right\} \qquad (v) + \ (vii) + \text{BUT ALTHOUGH (v) (i)}$$

$$(v) + (viii) + \text{ALTHOUGH} \left\{ \begin{array}{c} \text{HOWEVER} \\ \text{(v) (i)} \end{array} \right\} \qquad (v) + (viii) + \text{BUT ALTHOUGH (v) (i)}$$

(b) Combine the statements you have made in Exercise D with the following additional statements. For example:

> The couple who live together are usually legally married.
> The nuclear family is generally established by marriage.

> The nuclear family is usually established by a formal contract of marriage. THAT IS TO SAY, the couple who live together are usually legally married. . . . ALTHOUGH the nuclear family is generally established by marriage, HOWEVER, it can also be established by concubinage.

1. The husband may have to leave his family to work elsewhere.
   Some families are incomplete for economic reasons.
2. Most families in Britain would be nuclear families by this definition.
   The nuclear family may be defined as a man and a woman sharing a common residence with their offspring.
3. Most families are monogamous.
   Most families have one husband and one wife.
4. In Britain there are two main classes: the middle class and the working class.
   Western societies are stratified in terms of classes.
5. Most people in Britain know what is meant by class difference.
   The idea of social class is familiar.
6. People who are generally thought of as middle class tend to earn more than those who are commonly considered to be working class.
   Accountants and lawyers earn more than bus drivers and bricklayers.

There is a tendency for middle class people to earn more than people associated with the working class.

7. Ninety-five per cent of people in the survey who were asked what class these occupations were associated with said 'middle class'.
There was general agreement about the class of lawyers and accountants.

8. It provides for a sense of security and social integration.
Primary socialization has considerable importance.

9. They ought to support each other in preparing the individual for a useful place in society.
The two forms of socialization ought to complement each other.

10. Brahmans were traditionally priests and people belonging to the Kshatriya caste were traditionally warriors.
There is a traditional connection between certain castes and certain occupations.

11. There is no problem in deciding what caste a particular person belongs to.
The system appears to be very straightforward.

III GUIDED WRITING

EXERCISE F

Combine the following pairs of sentences into one by making use of the words in brackets. Replace expressions with pronouns where appropriate, and make any other necessary structural changes.

1. (a) Whichever view one takes, it seems clear that for satisfactory social learning to take place primary and secondary socialization need to be reconciled.
   (so that)
   (b) Primary and secondary socialization need to be complementary and not in conflict.

2. (a) Secondary socialization tends to have a wider frame of reference.
   (and)
   (b) Secondary socialization provides for the adaptation of the individual to a changing society.

3. (a) The change in social values is a necessary change.
   (which)
   (b) Education brings about a change in social values.

4. (a) Primary socialization, as we have defined primary socialization, tends to have a frame of reference which relates to the past.
   (and)

(b) Primary socialization, as we have defined primary socialization, provides for the learning of traditional values.
5. (a) Social change is, in some degree at least, a consequence of education. (and)
   (b) Secondary socialization has often been imposed on societies without regard to the importance of traditional values.

EXERCISE G

Arrange the sentences you have written in Exercise F into an appropriate order.

EXERCISE H

Form the sentences you have arranged in Exercise G into a paragraph by using the following expressions:

it can be argued, we might say, whereas, on the other hand, it can also be argued, and

The completed paragraph is a continuation of the reading passage in Section I.

IV   READING AND NOTE-TAKING

EXERCISE I   *Priming questions*

Read the following passage quickly to get a general idea of its contents. Bear these questions in mind.

1. How does language illustrate the possible conflict between primary and secondary socialization?
2. How do educationists propose to deal with this conflict?

It can be argued that the change in social values which education brings about is a necessary one. We might say that primary socialization, as we have defined it, tends to have a frame of reference which relates to the past and provides for the learning of traditional values, whereas secondary socialization tends to have a wider frame of reference and provides for the adaptation of the individual to a changing society. It can also be argued that social change is, in some degree at least, a consequence of education and secondary socialization has often been imposed on societies without regard to the importance of traditional values. Whichever view one takes, it seems clear that for satisfactory social learning to take place primary and secondary socialization need to be reconciled so that they are complementary and not in conflict.

Mention has already been made of the socializing function of language. In fact, language provides us with a good example of how primary and secondary socialization can come into conflict. The kind of language which the child uses at home or with his peer group, that is to say the other children in the neighbourhood who play with him, may be very different from the kind of language that his teacher expects him to use at school. The child may, for example, speak in a certain dialect which is not accepted as 'correct' by his teacher. In this case, the language behaviour of primary socialization is in conflict with the norms of language behaviour which are considered to be correct for the purposes of secondary socialization.

This problem is made more difficult by the fact that difference in the *kind* of language used at home and at school may go along with differences in the *uses* of language in these two situations. Language in the home, for example, may be used mainly for the purposes of interaction between the members of the family, as a way of maintaining emotional relationships. In the school classroom, however, the child is often required to use language in a different way. Here its purpose is not so much to help interaction as to serve as a means of acquiring and organizing knowledge. It serves an intellectual rather than an emotional purpose. In this case, conflict occurs because the uses of language developed in primary socialization are not those which are of primary importance in secondary socialization.

In view of these difficulties, some educationists have suggested the need for language programmes which will provide 'verbally deprived' children with the kind of language and its uses which they will need for their school education. Such a suggestion implies that priority should be given to secondary socialization. Other educationists have taken the contrary view. They believe that educational methods should themselves change so that they relate more closely to the child's experience, including his experience of language. To take this view is to argue that secondary socialization should adapt itself to primary socialization as far as possible and to imply that the latter should be given priority.

EXERCISE J *Notes*

Now read the passage more slowly and carefully and complete the following notes.

Paragraphs 2, 3   . . .   secondary socialization

language at home/with
peer group

language . . .

kind of language:	. . .	'correct'
use of language:	. . . emotional	acquisition of knowledge . . .

Paragraph 3

Solution (1)   Primary Secondary
               A   →   B
               priority given to . . .
               . . . socialization adapted to . . . socialization.

Solution (2)   Primary Secondary
               A   ←   B
               priority given to . . .
               . . . socialization adapted to . . . socialization.

DISCUSSION

Which of these solutions do you think is the better one?

4 Roles

1 READING AND COMPREHENSION

---

[1]The operation of a social group depends on its members having certain parts, or roles, to play. [2]Each member has a particular position in the structure of the group and has particular tasks to perform in its activity. [3]So his part carries with it certain obligations. [4]But it also gives him certain rights, since the performance of his tasks entitles him to receive services in return from other members of the group. [5]These sets of rights and obligations can be said to define the individual's social roles.

[6]Although the general notion of role is clear enough, there has in the past been considerable difference of opinion about how it should be given an exact definition. [7]A useful survey of different views on this matter is provided in Banton (1965). [8]After referring to the work of a number of scholars such as Linton (1936, 1947), Nadel (1957) and Merton (1957), Banton comes to the conclusion that in spite of differences of approach and emphasis there is enough general agreement among scholars working in the field at present to arrive at an agreed definition of the concept. [9]He expresses this as follows:

> [10]It is agreed: that behaviour can be related to a *position* in a social structure; that actual behaviour can be related to the individual's own ideas of what is appropriate (*role cognitions*), or to other people's ideas of what he *will* do (*expectations*), or to other people's ideas about what he *should* do (*norms*). [11]In this light a role may be understood as *a set of norms and expectations applied to the incumbent of a particular position.* (Banton 1965, pp. 28–9)

(a) *Individuals have certain rights and obligations as members of a group.*
(b) *An individual occupies a position in the structure of the group.* ·
(c) *Scholars are not in agreement about how the concept of role should be defined.*
(d) *Role cognitions refer to other people's ideas of what an individual's behaviour should be.*

[12]Although it is not clear from Banton's remarks what part the individual's own ideas play in defining role, nevertheless one may say that they reflect a

general agreement about how the concept of role is to be defined. [13]There is not the same consensus, however, on the question of how roles should be classified. [14]This is, of course, not surprising: different research purposes are likely to require classifications based on different criteria.

[15]Linton, in the works cited earlier, proposes a simple twofold classification. [16]He distinguishes ascribed roles from achieved roles. [17]The former are assigned to individuals by social custom by reference to such criteria as sex, age, kinship relations and caste. [18]Thus, for example, we might find that the rôle of hunter is an ascribed one in a particular society in that it is restricted to men of a certain age. [19]We might also find that when a man is too old to hunt he is automatically allocated another ascribed role – perhaps that of counsellor or priest. [20]Achieved roles, on the other hand, are those which the individual acquires by his own effort or by reason of certain personal qualities. [21]They are not bestowed upon him by social custom. [22]The role of president in the United States, for example, is achieved, whereas that of queen in Britain is ascribed.

[23]Linton's simple classification is a useful one. [24]The difference between caste and class systems of social stratification, for example, can be discussed by reference to ascribed and achieved roles. [25]The distinction also enters into discussions about the traditional roles of women in society. [26]Many women nowadays feel that they have roles ascribed to them and that they are prevented from acquiring other roles because these are only achieved roles for men.

REFERENCES

Banton, Michael (1965). *Roles: An Introduction to the Study of Social Relations.* London: Tavistock Publications.

Linton, Ralph (1936). *The Study of Man.* New York: Appleton Century Crofts.

——(1947). *The Cultural Background of Personality.* London: Routledge and Kegan Paul.

Merton, R. K. (1957). *Social Theory and Social Structure.* Glencoe, Illinois: Free Press.

Nadel, S. F. (1957). *The Theory of Social Structure.* London: Cohen and West.

SOLUTIONS

Complete the following statements by referring to the sentences of the passage which are indicated in brackets. Note that sometimes more than one word is required.

(a)   ... (1) of a group have certain roles to play.
     ... (5), as members of a group take on ... (3).
=   Individuals take on certain obligations as members of a group.

Individuals also have the . . . (4) to receive services in return.

∴ *Individuals have certain rights and obligations as members of a group.*

(b) Social structure consists of a number of . . . (2).
Each . . . (1) of a group occupies a certain position in the . . . (1) of the group.
. . . (5) occupy . . . (2) in the structure of the group.

= *An individual occupies a position in the structure of the group.*

(c) In the past, scholars have had different . . . (6) about the way to . . . (5) the concept of role.

= In the past, there was no . . . (8) on how the concept of role should be defined.
At present there is general agreement on the . . . (6) of the concept.

= Scholars *are* at present in general agreement about how the concept of role should be defined.

(d) Other people's ideas about what . . . (5) should do are referred to as . . . (10).

i.e. Norms refer to other people's ideas of what an individual's . . . (10) should be.
Role cognitions refer to the individual's own idea of . . . (10) behaviour.

= Role cognitions refer to the individual's *own* idea of what his behaviour should be.

EXERCISE A   *Meaning assessment*

Refer to the passage and:

(a) decide whether the following statements are true or false according to the passage.
(b) write out the true statement which expresses the most central idea.

Paragraph 1
1. Members of a social group have the obligation to carry out certain tasks.
2. An individual's social roles are defined by his rights and obligations.
3. An individual's rights are defined by the tasks he has to carry out.

Paragraph 2
1. The roles people play are defined by norms and expectations of behaviour.
2. A position in a social structure has certain norms of behaviour associated with it.
3. Role expectations refer to the way other people think an individual should behave.

Paragraph 4
1. Achieved roles are assigned by social custom.
2. Individuals can adopt roles by their own efforts.

3. Ascribed roles are restricted to certain members of a society.
4. Roles can be classified into two kinds: achieved and ascribed.
5. The role of hunter is an ascribed one.

EXERCISE B   *Contextual reference*

Refer to the relevant contexts in the reading passage and replace or expand
the expressions printed in italics with expressions which make the meaning
clear.

1. But *it* also gives *him* certain rights. (4)
2. A useful survey of different views on *this matter* is provided in Banton
   (1965). (7)
3. *He* expresses *this* as follows. (9)
4. Actual behaviour can be related to other people's ideas about what *he*
   should be. (10)
5. *This* is, of course, not surprising. (14)
6. *The former* are assigned to individuals by social custom. (17)
7. Achieved roles are *those* which the individual acquires by his own
   effort. (20)
8. *They* are not bestowed upon *him* by social custom. (21)
9. *The distinction* also enters into discussions about the traditional roles
   of women in society. (25)
10. *These* are only achieved roles for men. (26)

EXERCISE C   *Summary*

Write a summary of the reading passage by selecting one statement from
each group (a, b or c) which relates most appropriately to the numbered
statement and then by arranging all the statements in the most satisfactory
order. Your summary should be in two paragraphs.

1. Finally, role cognitions have to do with what the individual himself
   believes to be appropriate behaviour.
2. The position that individuals occupy has an effect on their behaviour.
   (a) This is related to role cognitions, norms and expectations.
   (b) Role cognitions refer to the individual's own idea about behaviour.
   (c) There is general agreement about how the concept should be defined.
3. Achieved roles, on the other hand, are acquired by the individual's own
   effort or because of his personal qualities.
   (a) The role of president in the United States, for example, is an achieved
   role.
   (b) Ascribed roles, on the other hand, are not acquired by the individual's
   own effort.
   (c) Achieved roles are earned, therefore, whereas ascribed roles are not.

4. One way of classifying roles is to distinguish between those which are ascribed and those which are achieved.
   (a) That is to say, achieved roles are not ascribed.
   (b) Ascribed roles are assigned to individuals by social custom.
   (c) Linton therefore proposed a simple classification.
5. Individuals have certain rights and obligations as members of a group, and they occupy positions in the structure of the group.
   (a) These refer to the individual's own idea about appropriate behaviour.
   (b) This set of rights and obligations associated with a particular position defines the individual's role.
   (c) Role is defined by reference to certain rights and obligations.
6. We may define role, then, as a set of norms and expectations associated with a particular position.
   (a) But although there is general agreement on definitions, there is less agreement on classification.
   (b) The positions which individuals occupy has an influence on their behaviour.
   (c) There is a difference of opinion about classification, but there is general agreement about definition.
7. Norms, for example, have to do with other people's ideas about what an individual's behaviour should be.
   (a) Such norms have an influence on behaviour.
   (b) Expectations, on the other hand, refer to what other people think an individual's behaviour *will* be.
   (c) How other people think an individual will behave depends on their expectation.

II   USE OF LANGUAGE

EXERCISE D   *Distinctions and definitions*

Look at Sentences 10 and 11 in the reading passage. They make a *distinction* between three kinds of influence on individual behaviour and provide a *definition* of each kind. We can show this as follows:

(a) Banton: influence on behaviour

Distinctions	role cognitions	norms	expectations
Definitions	individual's own ideas about appropriate behaviour	other people's ideas about what individual *should* do	other people's ideas about what individual *will* do

We can write these notes out to make a summary statement as follows:

(b) Banton makes a distinction between three kinds of influence on behaviour. He distinguishes between role cognitions, norms and expectations. Role cognitions refer to the individual's own ideas about appropriate behaviour, norms refer to other people's ideas about what the individual *should* do and expectations refer to their ideas about what they *will* do.

1. Write (a) notes and (b) a summary statement to show the distinctions and definitions relating to *role types* expressed in Sentences 1·5–26 of the reading passage.
2. Consider the following passages and write (a) notes and (b) summary statements as illustrated above.
   (i) Durkheim noticed that although suicide is in one respect a highly personal act, different societies have different but quite regular suicide rates. He therefore concluded that there must be social factors at work and set out to categorize different kinds of suicide with reference to the degree to which these social factors influenced the act. He used the term 'egoistic suicide' to refer to that kind of suicide which occurs when the individual is isolated, when the social bonds that link him to others are weakened or broken. 'Anomic suicide', on the other hand, occurs when there is a sudden change of accepted social norms or a breakdown of social values which normally regulate the individual's behaviour. The third kind of suicide is 'altruistic' and occurs when the individual's own identity is absorbed by the values of a particular social group and he acts to preserve those values.
   (ii) In most societies we find some kind of transmission of heritage. Either the roles or the possessions or both of members of one generation are handed down to the members of the next. Following Rivers, we can refer to the transmission of roles related to rank or office as 'succession' and the handing down of property as 'inheritance'.
   (iii) Bernstein speaks of the position-oriented family. This is one in which each member of the family acts out his allotted role: father, mother, son and so on. He compares this with what he calls the person-oriented family, in which the members of the family act more freely as individuals and in which the role structure is not precisely maintained. There is perhaps a tendency for position-oriented families to be more prevalent among the working class.
   (iv) Sympathetic magic operates on the principle that one event can influence another event at a distance by a kind of mysterious sympathy. Frazer, in his well-known work *The Golden Bough*, suggests that there are two branches of sympathetic magic. 'Homeopathic' or 'imitative' magic is that which is based on the belief that 'like produces like, or that an effect resembles its cause', and in this

case the magician supposes that he can produce any effect he wishes by imitating it. 'Contagious magic', on the other hand, is based on the belief that once there has been contact between two things this contact will remain afterwards. In this case, by doing something with an object which was once in contact with a person, a magician believes that he can affect the person himself.

(v) The folktales that are passed down from generation to generation, forming part of the 'cultural heritage' of a society, do not always have the same social function. Malinowski proposed a three-way classification and distinguished between myth, legend and fairy story. The first of these, he suggested, represents 'a statement of a higher and a more important truth of a primeval reality'. As such it is regarded as sacred. Fairy stories, on the other hand, are simply entertainment and nobody attaches any special significance to them, and nobody believes them to be true. Legends, however, are believed to be true historical accounts.

EXERCISE E   *Discourse development*

Relate each of the following groups of sentences into paragraphs by arranging them into an appropriate order and using the following expressions where necessary:

for example, on the other hand, however, that is to say

(Refer to *Use of Language* exercises in Units 1, 2 and 3.)

1. (a) Some families are polygynous.
   (b) In some societies we find polyandrous families.
   (c) The families consist of a woman and more than one husband.
   (d) The families consist of a man and more than one wife.
2. (a) Nuclear families may be incomplete because of economic necessity.
   (b) Many workers in Europe have to find work outside their own country.
3. (a) A family can exist when a couple shares a common residence.
   (b) A family exists when a man and a woman live together in one home.
4. (a) In India, a person born into the Kshatriya caste cannot move into a higher caste and become a Brahman.
   (b) In a caste system individuals cannot move from one social stratum to another.
   (c) A working class person can, if he has the opportunity, become middle class in the course of his life.
   (d) In a class system there is a greater degree of social mobility.
5. (a) Income is not a very reliable guide to social class.
   (b) One way of defining social class is by reference to income.
   (c) People in the teaching profession in Britain earn less than many people in occupations associated with the working class.

(d) We might define people earning a certain sum, say £2500 or less, as belonging to the working class.
6. (a) Secondary socialization provides for the individual's role in society as a whole.
   (b) Primary socialization provides for the individual's integration into the culture of his immediate environment.
   (c) Secondary socialization enables the individual to extend the range of his social activities.

III   GUIDED WRITING

EXERCISE F

Put the verbs in brackets in the following sentences into the correct form.

1. Banton (adopt) a rather different approach to role classification.
2. By this, Banton (mean) the degree to which roles (be) dependent on each other.
3. By this Banton (mean) the degree to which the adoption of one role (restrict) the individual's choice of other roles.
4. Those roles which (ascribe) on the basis of sex can (restrict) the individual's freedom (choose) other roles.
5. Banton (classify) them by reference to what he (call) differentiation.

6. Examples of independent roles would (be) leisure roles such as golfer or chess-player.
7. There (be) *independent roles*.
8. In this respect, sex roles (be) dependent and undifferentiated.
9. In many societies there (be) certain roles which cannot (adopt) by women.
10. Banton (call) roles of this kind *basic roles*.
11. Independent roles (be) highly differentiated.
12. Independent roles can (adopt) by any individual regardless of sex, age, religion, race or occupation.

13. Roles of this kind (be) more differentiated than basic roles.
14. Roles of this kind (be) differentiated less than independent roles.
15. An example of the third class might (be) the role of priest, or the role of policeman.
16. Banton also (suggest) a third class.
17. Banton (refer) to the third class as *general roles*.

EXERCISE G

Put the sentences you have written in Exercise F into an appropriate order within their groups. Begin with:

Banton adopts a rather different approach to role classification.

EXERCISE H

Form the groups of sentences you have arranged in Exercise G into a paragraph. Join sentences together to form single statements where appropriate by using relative clauses. For example:

16+17 Banton also suggests a third class, which he refers to as *general roles*.

Relate statements where appropriate by using the following expressions: *for example, thus, on the other hand.* The completed paragraph is a continuation of the reading passage.

IV   READING AND NOTE-TAKING

EXERCISE I   *Priming questions*

Read the following passage quickly to get a general idea of its contents. Bear these questions in mind:

1. What is meant by the relative independence of different roles?
2. Are roles the same in different societies?

Banton adopts a rather different approach to role classification. He classifies them by reference to what he calls differentiation. By this Banton means the degree to which the adoption of one role restricts the individual's choice of other roles, the degree to which roles are dependent on each other. Thus, those roles which are ascribed on the basis of sex can restrict the individual's freedom to choose other roles. In many societies, for example, there are certain roles which cannot be adopted by women. In this respect, sex roles are dependent and undifferentiated. Banton calls roles of this kind *basic roles*. On the other hand, there are *independent roles*, which are highly differentiated and which can be adopted by any individual regardless of sex, age, religion, race or occupation. Examples of these would be leisure roles such as golfer or chess-player. Banton also suggests a third class, which he refers to as *general roles*, an example of which might be the role of priest, or the role of policeman. Roles of this kind are differentiated less than independent roles but more than basic ones.

Banton proposes that we might classify particular roles in a society by locating them on a scale with basic roles at one end, independent roles at the other and general roles in the middle. He illustrates this by means of the following diagram:

	s	a		o		l		

0 ├──────┼──────┼────────────┼──────────────┼──────┤ 100

basic roles   general roles   independent
                                                                 roles

s = sex roles   a = age roles   o = occupational roles   l = leisure roles

The diagram is intended to show the relative independence of different roles. The roles at the left-hand side of the scale restrict the behaviour of their incumbents, and so their freedom to adopt other roles at will, more than those which are nearer the right-hand end of the scale. As Banton puts it:

> 'This scale compares the extent to which particular roles can be played independently of other roles. A person's sex role usually affects the way people respond to him or her more than does any other role; it is relevant to conduct in a wide range of situations. A person's occupation affects the way others behave towards him or her at a social gathering but has less influence than his or her sex. A leisure role – like golfer – has few implications outside the golf club.' (Banton 1965, p. 33.)

The locating of different kinds of role on the scale will, of course, vary from society to society. Thus, as Banton points out, in pre-literate societies we will find that sex and age roles are less differentiated and so more dependent than they are in industrial societies. They will therefore be located further to the left of the scale. Another difference between industrial societies and pre-literate societies is that in the former there is a large number of general and independent roles. These, again, can be located on different points of the scale with reference to their degree of independence. The occupational role of priest, for example, leaves the incumbent with less freedom of choice to adopt other roles than does that of policeman. The leisure role of golfer is more independent than the role of student, which, as an occupational role, is much less restricted and much more differentiated than that of policeman. In other words, being a golfer does not prevent the incumbent from being all kinds of other things as well. The role of student is slightly more restrictive. That of policeman is even more restrictive in that the incumbent is not free to take on any other roles at will. The priest, of course, has even less social liberty of this kind.

EXERCISE J   *Notes*

1. The way in which different roles vary in independence in industrial and pre-literate societies is illustrated by Banton by use of the following scales. Complete the scales by reference to the passage.

Pre-literate societies

```
             s     a        ?          ?
0 ├──────────┴─────┴────────┴──────────┴──────────┤ 100
```

Industrial societies

```
                s a   ?   ?           ?     ?
0 ├───────────┴─┴───┴───┴──────────┴─────┴──┤ 100
  basic roles          general roles        independent roles
```

s = sex roles	p = priest
a = age roles	pc = policeman
o = occupational roles	st = student
l = leisure roles	g = golfer

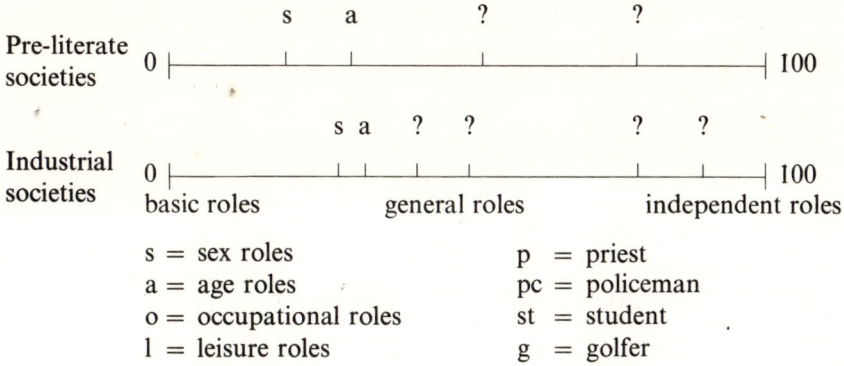

2. Now label the position on the scales with reference to the information given.

    (a) Society A: hunter (h) – restricted to men – certain age – special code of conduct
         farmer (f) – unrestricted

```
0 ├──────────────┴───────────────┴──────────────────┤ 100
  basic roles                              independent roles
```

    (b) Society B: schoolteachers (st) – free to enter politics – university teachers (ut) – status of civil servants – not allowed to enter politics – regulations about publishing articles, extra earnings, etc.

```
0 ├───────────────────────┴──────────┴───────────────┤ 100
  basic roles                              independent roles
```

DISCUSSION

Do you think Banton's approach to the classification of roles is a valid one? What would be the relative positions on the Banton scale of the following roles in your own society?

schoolteacher, politician, soldier, tradesman, banker, religious leader, policeman.

5 Population

I READING AND COMPREHENSION

[1]In 1974 the population of the world increased by the staggering total of 74 million people. [2]Those 74 million had the distinction of arriving in the year when the world's enormously expanded, and still rapidly increasing, population was officially declared to be a problem by the United Nations. [3]The proclamation of World Population Year in 1974 was welcome evidence that more and more governments are prepared to admit that some form of family planning is now a universal need.

[4]We know that the world's population has been increasing steadily ever since the beginning of historical records. [5]In recent years, however, this increase has been particularly large. [6]In many countries at the present time population explosions are being experienced such as have never been known in all history. [7]The population of the world is estimated to have been 5 million in 8000 B.C. [8]From archaeological evidence and some surviving census figures we are able to estimate the world's population at between 200 and 300 million at the beginning of the first century A.D. [9]More definite figures become possible with the accumulation of historical material on a large scale. [10]By A.D. 1650 there were 500 million people in the world. [11]By 1850 the population was 1000 million. [12]It had doubled again by 1930 to 2000 million, and it had doubled yet again by 1975 to 4000 million.

(a) *The proclamation of World Population Year can be regarded as a significant step forward in the campaign for universal family planning.*

(b) *We do not possess the means of estimating world population figures much before the seventeenth century* A.D.

[13]Demographers, or population statisticians, are alarmed less by the absolute rise in world population numbers than by the increase in the rate of growth. [14]This can be demonstrated by considering how long it takes the population of the world to double. [15]A man living in 1650 could expect it to take 200 years to double the population of the world. [16]Starting from 1850 it took 80 years and from 1930 only 45 years. [17]Starting from 1975 we can expect the population of the world to double in about 35 years.

[18]It is not easy to find solutions to problems caused by population growth of this magnitude. [19]In part, effective action is lacking because of our in-

ability to decide exactly where the problems lie. [20]For example, many millions of people do not have enough to eat, but at the same time one could argue that the world is not over-populated with respect to its food supply at the present time. [21]The total cultivable land is more than 15,000 million acres. [22]With the present population of about 4000 million, this means there are between 3·5 and 4 acres per person. [23]Using modern agricultural methods, we can produce food for one person on 1·3 acres. [24]It appears, then, that the world's population could be almost three times as large before there was a serious shortage of food. [25]But it is unlikely that all the arable land would be used for food production. [26]If this were the case there would be no land left to meet man's increasing demand for houses, factories, airports, roads and recreation facilities.

(c) *Demographers can show that the world's population is doubling more and more quickly.*

(d) *Assuming between 3·5 and 4 acres of land per person, we could argue that our food supply is inadequate.*

[27]It is widely believed that the world's population has exploded because infant mortality has been reduced and the average length of life extended on a dramatic scale. [28]Yet three-quarters of the world's people remain convinced that they must have many children in order that a few may survive. [29]The result has been a fast-expanding population in most parts of the world, with an unusually large proportion of young people. [30]For example, more than half the people of India today are under 18. [31]This means that if, by a miracle, the birthrate in India could be limited to what is termed replacement level, i.e. an average of just over two children to each couple, the population would continue to grow for at least another generation. [32]If it were possible to cut the birthrate below the replacement level this would produce a maladjusted age distribution, with far more old people than young, and the new situation might bring on more calamities of its own.

[33]The best hope, then, seems to be a stable world population maintained at the level it will have reached some time in the twenty-first century, which would certainly be at a level twice as high as it was in 1975. [34]Pessimists, on the other hand, expect an accelerating upward trend until the limits of food, space and natural resources impose their own crude answers.

(e) *The problem of rapid population growth in India could not be solved quickly even if people limited themselves to an average of just over two children per couple.*

(f) *It is reasonably certain that eventually the population of the world will stabilize at a level of about 8000 million.*

SOLUTIONS

Complete the following statements by referring to the passage above.

(a) The . . . was an official admission on the part of . . . that rapid . . . growth constitute a serious . . . . It showed that many . . . all over the world are prepared to think about the need for . . . .

∴ *The proclamation of World Population Year can be regarded as a signifi-cant step forward in the campaign for universal family planning.*

(b) By A.D. 1650 enough . . . has accumulated to allow us to make a fairly accurate assessment of . . . at that time. However, historians have succeeded in estimating world population on the basis of . . . and . . . as early as the first century A.D.

∴ We have the means of estimating world population figures well before the seventeenth century A.D.

(c) Population statisticians can . . . the increase in . . . by considering how long it takes for . . . . Starting from . . . it took 200 years to . . . . Starting from . . . it took 80 years, and from 1930 . . . .

∴ *Demographers can show that the world's population is doubling more and more quickly.*

(d) The present . . . is about 4000 million, and there are more than 15,000 million areas of . . . . In other words, there are between . . . . Since, using . . . , we can produce . . . on 1·3 acres, we could argue that there would not be a serious . . . until there were . . . as many people.

∴ Assuming between 3·5 and 4 acres of land per person, we could *not* argue that our food supply is inadequate.

(e) As a result of rapid population growth, more than . . . are under 18. Even if the . . . could be . . . level, the population would continue to grow for at least . . . .

∴ *The problem of rapid population growth in India could not be solved quickly even if people limited themselves to an average of just over two children per couple.*

(f) Some experts hope that during the twenty-first century a . . . will be achieved at a level . . . as it was in 1975. In 1975 the world population was about . . . ; twice that equals . . . . Less optimistic observers, however, expect the . . . to continue until the world runs out of . . . .

∴ It is by no means certain that the population of the world will stabilize at a level of about 8000 million.

EXERCISE A   *Meaning assessment and summary writing*

1. Refer to the passage and decide whether the following statements are true or false.

   (a) Until recently many of the world's governments have been reluctant to admit the need for family planning.

   (b) It is reasonable to assume that in time all arable land will be fully utilized by modern farming methods.

   (c) A majority of the world's people still believe they must have many children to allow for the fact that some may die in infancy.

(d) Demographers expect that India will soon succeed in limiting the birthrate to replacement level.

(e) If we succeeded in drastically reducing the birthrate, we would end up with a population containing more old people than young, thus perhaps giving rise to as many problems as we had solved.

(f) The large proportion of young people resulting from the increased birthrate means that the world's population must continue to grow for at least another generation.

(g) The absence of historical evidence means that we have no means of estimating the world's population in ancient times.

(h) It is far from easy to determine the point at which a population becomes too large.

2. Why has it proved so difficult to tackle the world population problem? Write an answer to this question, using the true statements above. Write a paragraph containing five sentences with additional material as follows:

(a) ...
(b) This may have been due partly to the fact that ...
(c) Another difficulty is that ...
(d) ...
(e) On the other hand ...

EXERCISE B *Contextual reference*

Refer to the context in which the following sentences appear and replace or expand the expressions printed in italics so as to make the meaning clear.

1. *It* had doubled again by 1930 to 2000 million. (12)
2. *This* can be demonstrated by considering how long it takes the population of the world to double. (14)
3. Starting from 1850 *it* took 80 years and from 1930 only 45 years. (16)
4. *The total cultivable land* is more than 15,000 million acres. (21)
5. With the present population of about 4000 million, *this* means there are between 3·5 and 4 acres per person. (22)
6. If *this were the case* there would be no land left to meet man's increasing demand for houses, factories, airports, roads and recreation facilities. (26)

EXERCISE C *Relationships between statements*

Link the following statements together to form a paragraph by using the logical connectors given below. The statements are already in the right order, but in (13) *originate* should be changed to *originating*.

but, for example, moreover, because, therefore, on the other hand, and

1. Population pressure results from an imbalance between population and resources.
2. Man's needs are socially conditioned and vary from country to country.

3. A child in Northern Europe may consume twenty times as much as a child born in India.
4. He has been conditioned to expect a relatively high standard of living.
5. The European child 'needs' twenty times as much in raw materials.
6. We cannot determine what constitutes an optimum population figure simply by comparing the existing population densities in different countries.
7. Holland and the United States are both technologically advanced countries.
8. Holland has eighteen times the population density of the United States.
9. The United States could not support such a density of population with her economy organized as at present.
10. The United States produces a high proportion of her own food and raw materials.
11. Her imports of these essential commodities are relatively small.
12. Holland's imports are enormous.
13. No less than 85% of Holland's resources originate from outside her own borders.

II   USE OF LANGUAGE

EXERCISE D   *Combining two sentences by means of a relative clause (i)*

Look at the following examples:

(a) A person . . . is likely to stand out among his colleagues. *This person* has a special talent of some sort.
    A person *who* has a special talent of some sort is likely to stand out among his colleagues.
(b) The two social movements . . . have reached the stage of formal organization. We have analysed *these two movements* in the above section.
    The two social movements *which* we have analysed in the above section have reached the stage of formal organization.

In each of the examples above, two sentences have been combined into a single sentence, using a *defining relative clause*. The purpose of this is to tell us what person, or what two social movements, we are talking about.

Now compare the following:

(c) Mr R, who has a special talent for organizing, works in the personnel department.

In example (c) we know who we are talking about – Mr R. The clause *who has a special talent for organizing* tells us something more about Mr R. It is a *non-defining relative clause*. Non-defining relative clauses are often written with commas, but not always.

In (a) and (c) *who* refers to a person. In (b) *which* refers to a thing.

Combine each of the following pairs of sentences into a single sentence. Make the second sentence into a relative clause and insert it into the first sentence at the place marked by dots. State whether the relative clauses are defining or non-defining. For example:

A person who has a special talent of some sort is likely to stand out among his colleagues. (*defining*)

Mr R, who has a special talent for organizing, works in the personnel department. (*non-defining*)

1. Unlike the middle-class careerist, . . . , the average manual worker has a limited occupational horizon. The middle-class careerist thinks in long-range terms.
2. Some regulations are impossible to enforce because they are broken by so many people . . . . These people are otherwise law-abiding citizens.
3. Psychoanalysts have discovered that even well-adjusted people possess some wishes . . . . They would hesitate to disclose these wishes even to their closest friends.
4. Department stores prosecute very few of the women . . . . These women are caught shoplifting every day.
5. The philosophical controversy over free will versus determinism . . . cannot be regarded as finally settled. This controversy has been waged for over two thousand years.
6. The legislators and judges . . . must assess various power interests and attempt to strike a balance. The legislators and judges make the law in any given society.
7. In all times and in all places most men have been conservative, in that they have clung to the moral norms and social values . . . . These norms and values have come down to them from the past.
8. In an automated system the machines . . . are checked by other machines . . . The machines do the work. The machines guide the flow of materials and keep records of output.

EXERCISE E *Combining two sentences by means of a relative clause (ii)*

Look at the following sentences:

(a) One of the most important mechanisms . . . is imitation. Learning takes place *through these mechanisms*.
   One of the most important mechanisms *through which* learning takes place is imitation.
(b) Children . . . often feel insecure. *The parents of these children* give them no companionship.
   Children *whose parents* give them no companionship often feel insecure.

In (a) Preposition + Noun Phrase becomes Preposition + *which*. In (b) *The* + Noun + Possessive becomes *whose* + Noun.

Combine each of the following pairs of sentences into a single sentence. Make the second sentence into a relative clause and insert it into the first sentence at the place marked by dots. State whether the relative clauses are defining or non-defining.

1. The Zuni, . . . , frown on anyone trying to exalt himself above others. The culture of the Zuni is organized to prevent too much competition.
2. Modern criminal law is regarded as the area . . . . In this area the state inflicts punishment on persons guilty of prescribed offences.
3. There are certain types of criminal behaviour . . . . Organized society looks with particular disfavour on these types of behaviour.
4. There were seventy-five families in the United States in 1935–6 . . . . The average income of these families was $2,000,000.
5. In a complex society the groups . . . may not command our undivided loyalty, as do those in primitive society. We happen to belong to these groups.
6. In the early days of the factory system, workers . . . often reacted with violence. The jobs of these workers were replaced by machines.
7. A man . . . may have a series of in-group and out-group relationships with the same individuals. The friends of this man belong to other groups.
8. The division of labour is a common principle of social organization. According to this principle some people supervise and others are directed.

EXERCISE F   *Writing paragraphs based on population profiles*

1. Refer to Figure 1 and complete the paragraph which follows.

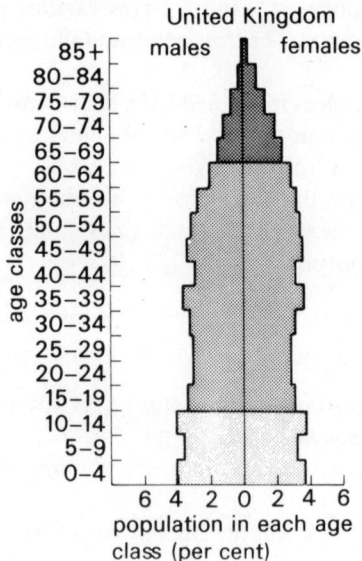

FIGURE 1   *Age composition of the United Kingdom, 1959*

(From Paul R. Ehrlich & Anne H. Ehrlich (1972) *Population, Resources, Environment: Issues in Human Ecology*, 2nd ed., San Francisco, W. H. Freeman & Co. Copyright © 1972.)

The population profile in Figure 1 shows the . . . of the . . . . In the year
. . . about . . . % of the total population were under 15 years of age. About
. . . % were aged 65 or older. Therefore about . . . % of the population were
economically dependent. The age class 15–64 represented . . . % of the
population. It follows that the ratio of productive to non-productive
members was roughly two to . . . . The narrow, even profile reflects the
United Kingdom's low birthrate and low . . . . As in most developed
countries, the death rate does not increase until the decade between the
ages of 55 to . . . .

2. Refer to Figure 2 and complete the paragraph below.

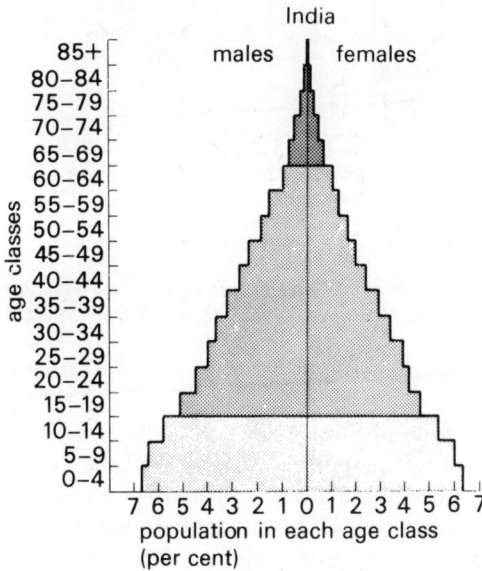

FIGURE 2   *Age composition of India, 1951*

(From Paul R. Ehrlich & Anne H. Ehrlich (1972) *Population, Resources, Environment: Issues in
Human Ecology*, 2nd ed., San Francisco, W. H. Freeman & Co. Copyright © 1972.)

Figure 2 is a . . . which shows . . . . In the year . . . about 37% of the total
population were . . . . About 6% were . . . . Therefore about . . . % of the
population were . . . . The economically active age class . . . represented
. . . % of the population. It follows that the ratio of productive to non-
productive members was . . . . The wide base of the profile reflects India's
high . . . . About . . . % of the population were in the age class 0–4 and
about . . . % in the age class 5–9. About . . . % were 10–14 years of age.

3. Refer to Figure 3 and write a paragraph describing the age composition
of Japan in 1960. Refer to paragraphs 1 and 2 as necessary. Note that the
relatively narrow base of the profile is due to a sharp decrease in the birthrate.

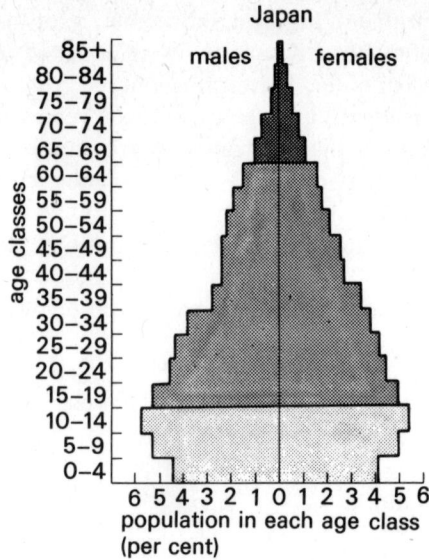

FIGURE 3   *Age composition of Japan, 1960*

(From Paul R. Ehrlich & Anne H. Ehrlich (1972) *Population, Resources, Environment: Issues in Human Ecology*, 2nd ed., San Francisco, W. H. Freeman & Co. Copyright © 1972.)

4. Complete the following paragraph comparing information from Figures 1 and 2.

   India's wide triangular profile is typical of many ... countries. In contrast, the United Kingdom's ... profile is typical of the developed countries. About ... % of India's population is under 15 years of age compared with about ... % of the United Kingdom's population. In other words, India has proportionately ... % more children. But the United Kingdom has proportionately ... % more people aged 65 or older than India. Therefore the age class 65 to 85 and above is ... as large in the population of the United Kingdom. The diagrams show that ... % of the United Kingdom's population is economically active compared with ... % of India's population. The ratio of productive to non-productive people in the United Kingdom is ... and in India .... We can conclude that the age class ... carried a heavier economic burden in India.

5. Using information from Figures 1 and 3, write a paragraph comparing the age composition of the United Kingdom and Japan. Refer to paragraph 4 as necessary. Note that Japan's profile for groups under the age of 15 is that of a developed country and for groups of 15 and over that of an underdeveloped country.

III   GUIDED WRITING

EXERCISE G

Study the following notes for a paragraph on the ideas of Robert Malthus. The notes are arranged in ten groups, and each group corresponds to a sentence in the paragraph. Join each group of notes into one sentence, using the additional material in brackets. Make any other changes that you think are necessary. Be careful about articles, tenses and punctuation. For example:

> Robert Malthus was an English clergyman – he was also a political economist – population of the world tends to increase fast – food supply increases more slowly (and, who believed that, faster than)

= *Robert Malthus was an English clergyman and a political economist who believed that the population of the world tends to increase faster than the food supply.*

Now do the others in the same way.

1. Mankind fails to control birth rate – poverty and war will result – these processes will bring about natural restriction (if, and, of the increase).
2. Malthus claimed – four children in first generation – 16 in second generation – 64 in third generation (that if, there were, there might be, and, and so on).
3. Fertility rate constant – population increases (assuming that, remains, by geometric progression).
4. Total numbers increase very rapidly – series reaches certain point – rate factor remains same (after, even though).
5. Food increases – 2, 4, 6, 8, 10, 12 (arithmetical, such as, in, series).
6. Malthus talked about food – he meant land – people grow food (when, really, where, could).
7. Always plenty of land – we might hope – food supply increase like population (if there was, then, that, would, indefinitely).
8. Malthus lived at end of eighteenth century – people could increase food supply – add more land to cultivated areas – amount of land limited (and, at that time, only if, and).
9. Situation was a race – birthrate – food (as Malthus saw it, increasing, supply of).

EXERCISE H

Check that you have ten good sentences, including the example at the beginning. Make sure you know all the words, using a dictionary if necessary. The sentences are already in the right order, but to make a good paragraph you will have to add some logical connectors. Look again at your ten sentences and decide where the following connectors can be inserted:

consequently
thus
this means that
on the other hand
however
therefore

Write a final version of the entire paragraph.

IV   READING AND NOTE-TAKING

EXERCISE I   *Priming questions*

Read the following passage quickly to get a general idea of its contents. Find and write out the answers to the following questions:

1. Why is the death rate falling in many countries?
2. What effect does industrialization have on the birthrate?
3. Why do official attitudes to population growth vary?

Even if we could determine the right size of population for a given country, such a balance would not be easy to achieve. The rate of population growth is fastest in technologically underdeveloped countries. In many of these countries a high birthrate is accompanied by a deathrate which has been lowered by modern drugs and improved standards of public health. Ideally it should be possible to counterbalance the effect of a reduced death rate by an increased use of family planning. In practice, however, population control is a highly complex matter which involves more than the availability of contraceptive devices. Throughout history people have determined the size of their families, whether large or small, according to the cultural values of the society in which they live.

Population control, then, is socially as well as biologically determined. For example, it is known that voluntary family planning programmes do not become effective until after the population has begun to fall. This finding is not as paradoxical as it seems. As living standards rise, a large family is no longer necessary as an insurance against the future. Consequently, birthrates may begin to fall independently of any official family planning campaign. In some cases, a downward shift in population seems to come about automatically as a society develops industrially. If eventually the whole world passes through the transition from an agricultural to a modern industrial economy, can we assume that birthrates will fall to manageable levels without the imposition of enforced family planning? Again there is a problem, since many economists doubt whether there are enough resources in the world for the necessary level of industrial development to be achieved universally.

The advantages and disadvantages of a large population have long been a subject of discussion among economists. On the one hand it has been argued that the supply of good agricultural land is limited. In order to feed a large population, inferior land must be cultivated and the good land worked very intensively. As a result, each person produces less in a given amount of time and this means a lower average income than could be obtained with a smaller population. Other economists have argued that a large population gives more scope for specialization and the development of facilities such as ports, roads and railways, which are not likely to be built unless there is a big demand to justify them. Similarly, it can be argued that many of the overhead costs of society, such as those involved in providing the basic framework of government, are less burdensome to each individual if they are shared among the members of a large population.

One of the difficulties in implementing a world-wide birth control programme lies in the fact that official attitudes to population growth vary from country to country depending on the level of industrial development and the availability of food and raw materials. In one of the under-developed countries where a vastly expanded population is pressing hard upon the limits of food, space and natural resources, it will be the first concern of government to place a limit on the birthrate, whatever the consequences may be. In a highly industrialized society the problem may be more complex. A declining birthrate may lead to unemployment because it results in a diminishing market for manufactured goods. Cities with a declining population may have to face the prospect of a shrinking tax base and perhaps a fall in land values. If there are fewer children going to school teachers may be thrown out of work. When the pressure of population on housing declines, prices also decline and the building industry, with its many ramifications throughout the economy, is weakened. Faced with considerations such as these, the government of a developed country may well prefer to see a slowly increasing population, rather than one which is stable or in decline.

EXERCISE J   *Notes*

Now read the passage more slowly and carefully and think about the main points in each paragraph.

Below there are eight statements based on the passage. Write out the statements in the correct order so that they summarize the most important points in each paragraph. Arrange your notes in four sections to correspond to the four paragraphs. Within each section, make the relationship between the statements clear by using the expressions *on the one hand, on the other hand, however*.

1. This is not an answer to overpopulation, since it is not likely that the whole world will become highly industrialized.
2. A large population gives more scope for specialization, for providing transport systems and for spreading the burden of government.
3. Family size is generally determined by cultural as well as biological factors.
4. A small population may mean higher productivity and a higher average income.
5. In an underdeveloped country with a large population, the most important concern is to reduce the birthrate.
6. In theory a lower deathrate could be matched by a lower birthrate if everyone used birth control methods.
7. A developed country may prefer a slowly rising birthrate in order to maintain employment, land values and revenue.
8. Often, when a country develops industrially, living standards rise and the birthrate tends to fall.

DISCUSSION

Do you agree with the author of the first reading passage that the governments of the world are beginning to take the problem of overpopulation seriously?

6 Migration

---

[1]Migration may be defined as a permanent change of residence by an individual or a group. [2]This definition is not entirely satisfactory, since it leaves us with the problem of deciding what is permanent. [3]In studies of international migration a person is usually classed as an immigrant if he has stated his intention of settling in the host country for at least a year.

[4]One form of migration is found when workers and their families cross national boundaries in search of better employment than is available at home. [5]Labour migration on a large scale, often involving a permanent or semi-permanent resettlement of the worker and his family, was a major factor in the economic expansion of Western Europe after the end of the Second World War. [6]By 1960 migrant workers from Portugal, Yugoslavia, Greece, Turkey and many other countries were to be found building houses, staffing hospitals, mending roads and manning assembly-lines everywhere in the industrial cities of the north. [7]It was estimated in 1975 that in the Common Market countries one in every sixteen workers was a foreigner. [8]The flow of migrant workers fluctuates according to the state of the economy in the host countries, but if recent trends continue the immigrant labour force in Western Europe could soon reach a total of 22 million. [9]This would be half as many people as emigrated from Europe to the New World in the nineteenth and early twentieth centuries.

(a) *If present trends continue, migrant workers are likely to become increasingly important to the economy of the Common Market.*

[10]Although an abundant supply of foreign labour has become essential to the West European economy, the influx of large numbers of foreigners has given rise to a variety of social problems. [11]If large numbers of foreigners are present they tend to put pressure on jobs, housing and education. [12]Because their standard of living is often low compared with other groups of workers, they crowd together in the slums. [13]Above all, they give rise to fears among the native population. [14]Thus, in many countries concern has been expressed about the dangers of 'foreignization'. [15]If the immigrants become too numerous, if they establish themselves too rapidly, or come

from too far away, they may pass what sociologists call the 'threshold of tolerance'.

[16]According to E. J. B. Rose, the migration of workers to the United Kingdom in recent times has been influenced more by the demand for labour in Britain than by unfavourable conditions at home. [17]The rate of immigration to Britain increased in 1955 and 1960, when there was an expanding industrial base. [18]It declined from 1956 to 1958 when the labour market was saturated. [19]Exceptions to this pattern are the political refugees and the rush of immigrants prior to the enactment of the Commonwealth Immigration Act in 1962.

(b) *It is rarely the case that immigrants cause fears among the native population.*

(c) *Past experience has shown that the rate of immigration to Britain increases when the demand for labour increases.*

[20]British society is relatively stable, homogeneous and egalitarian. [21]Consequently it exerts considerable pressure towards overall uniformity. [22]On the other hand, it does permit some degree of cultural plurality, as the success of the immigrant Jewish community indicates. [23]Of the immigrants who have arrived since 1939, the Poles, greatly aided by an official reception and resettlement programme, have been the most completely assimilated. [24]Some West Indians have readily adapted to their new country since they are largely English-speaking Christians and come from a British-oriented culture. [25]Eastern European political exiles also share a Christian heritage with the host country and have a similar culture, but they do not become assimilated to the same extent because many of them hope eventually to return home.

[26]Some immigrant groups, permanently settled in Britain, do not choose to integrate with British society. [27]These are said by sociologists to be self-segregating. [28]Examples of self-segregating groups are the Indian and Pakistani communities which have established themselves in Britain during the last thirty years. [29]In these groups, a distinct language and culture (including religion) are maintained by means of a tight internal organization. [30]Because such communities seek a measure of cultural plurality greater than the host country has historically accorded to any group, the result has been an increase in social tension.

(d) *If an immigrant has a similar language or culture to the people in the host country he will quickly be assimilated.*

(e) *A self-segregating community is one which chooses to maintain its own language and culture.*

(f) *The establishment of a self-segregating immigrant community may lead to social tension.*

SOLUTIONS

Complete the following statements by referring to the passage above.

(a) Migrant workers are so important to the . . . of the . . . countries that in 1975 one out of every sixteen workers was a . . . . If migrant workers . . . to come as they do at the . . . time, their numbers could soon reach . . . .

∴ *If present trends continue, migrant workers are likely to become increasingly important to the economy of the Common Market.*

(b) When large numbers of foreigners . . . together, they cause fears among . . . , who are afraid of . . . . Concern about this problem has been expressed . . . .

i.e. It is often the case that immigrants cause fears among the native population.

(c) The industrial base of Britain . . . in 1955 and 1960. These favourable conditions created a . . . , and the . . . increased in response to this demand.

i.e. Past experience has shown that the rate of immigration to Britain increases when the demand for labour increases.

(d) Coming from a British-oriented . . . , the West Indians speak . . . and a large number of them are . . . . Consequently they have been readily . . . . However, although Eastern European . . . are . . . to the native population in religion and . . . generally they tend not to be assimilated so . . . .

∴ It is not necessarily true that if an immigrant has a similar language or culture to the people in the host country he will quickly be assimilated.

(e) Some immigrant groups do not want . . . . In these cases the members of the group maintain . . . . Such communities are said to be . . . .

i.e. A self-segregating community is one which chooses to maintain its own language and culture.

(f) The Indian and Pakistani communities in Britain are examples of . . . groups. Experience has shown that the establishment of such . . . has sometimes led to an increase in . . . .

i.e. The establishment of a self-segregating immigrant community may lead to social tension.

EXERCISE A   *Meaning assessment and summary writing*

1. Refer to the passage and decide whether the following statements are true or false.
   (a) There are now a very large number of foreign workers in the industrial cities of Western Europe.
   (b) In the Common Market countries in 1975 it was estimated that one-third of the labour force consisted of immigrant labour.
   (c) The economy of the Common Market could not have expanded so rapidly without an abundant supply of foreign labour.
   (d) The foreign workers put pressure on housing, jobs and education, and the native population are beginning to fear the effects of 'foreignization'.

(e) There is little reason to suppose that the immigrants in Western Europe will pass the 'threshold of tolerance'.

(f) Labour migration to Western Europe has been common since the end of the Second World War.

(g) The flow of migrant workers into Western Europe remains constant and is not noticeably affected by the state of the economy.

(h) The migrant workers have had a good effect on the economy, but at the same time they have given rise to a variety of social problems.

2. Have migrant workers been of benefit to the countries of Western Europe? Write an answer to this question, using the true statements above in a different order. Write a passage containing five sentences, with additional material as follows:

(a) . . .

(b) Undoubtedly . . .

(c) However . . .

(d) The result is that they . . .

(e) Thus, . . .

EXERCISE B   *Contextual reference*

Refer to the context in which the following sentences appear and replace or expand the expressions printed in italics so as to make the meaning clear.

1. *This definition* is not entirely satisfactory, since it leaves us with the problem of deciding what is permanent. (2)
2. *This* would be half as many people as emigrated from Europe to the New World in the nineteenth and early twentieth centuries. (9)
3. Because *their* standard of living is often low compared with other groups of workers, they crowd together in the slums. (12)
4. Above all, *they* give rise to fears among the native population. (13)
5. *It* declined from 1956 to 1958 when the labour market was saturated. (18)
6. On the other hand, *it* does permit some degree of cultural plurality. (22)
7. In *these groups*, a distinct language and culture (including religion) are maintained by means of a tight internal organization. (29)

EXERCISE C   *Relationships between statements*

Link the following statements together to form a paragraph by using the logical connectors given below. The statements are already in the right order.

and, which, furthermore, for example, nevertheless

1. It is difficult to determine to what extent racial discrimination accounts for immigrant housing patterns in Britain.
2. Much statistical work remains to be done.
3. It is a formidable task of interpretation to isolate any one factor as predominant.
4. Some 72% of non-white immigrants in Britain live in the conurbations of London, the West Midlands, South-east Lancashire, West Yorkshire, Merseyside and Tyneside.
5. In many of these areas immigrants and indigenous people alike suffer from the poor quality of housing.
6. Some 47% of the immigrants live in London.
7. London has had a shortage of housing since 1949.
8. The picture in London is distorted by the number of substantial Victorian terrace houses suitable for multiple occupation.
9. It is quite clear that immigrants have a higher housing density than native British people.
10. They also occupy more shared accommodation, pay more and have less choice than native British people.

II   USE OF LANGUAGE

EXERCISE D   *The impersonal passive*

The impersonal passive is very common in formal writing. Examine the following active and passive sentences, and note that passive sentences contain some form of the verb *to be* together with a past participle:

Active	*Passive*
We often discuss society.	Society is often discussed.
We often discussed society.	Society was often discussed.
We may often discuss society.	Society may often be discussed.
Sociologists have often discussed society.	Society has often been discussed (by sociologists).

Note that the prepositional phrase in brackets is optional and is often omitted.

Rewrite the following sentences, changing the verb in italics into the passive, and making whatever other changes may be necessary. Words in brackets should be omitted in the rewritten sentences. For example:

(We) *can explain* the universality of religion by the important social functions it serves.

The universality of religion can be explained by the important social functions it serves.

1. In most preliterate societies, (people) *expect* all mature members to be proficient at duties common to their sex.
2. Certain targets of prejudice remain constant, but (people) *aim at* them far less often than was the case a few decades ago.
3. (The members of the tribe) *extended* the incest taboo beyond blood relationship to include all affinal kin, if they customarily shared close residence.
4. Nowadays it would be difficult to find an activity that the government *does not* more or less *supervise* and more or less *control*.
5. (People) *have deplored* conflict in almost all times and places, and yet it occurs in all times and places. (We) *can explain* this by the inevitable clash within groups and societies and between groups and societies.
6. In a typically large household, a large number of relatives *surrounded* the children.
7. (People) often *ask* sociologists a question which (they) seldom *put* to scientists in other fields. If sociology cannot solve the problems of society, what good is sociology?
8. (Some authors) *have described* culture in terms of universality and variability; (they) *have also defined* it as being transmitted from one generation to the next.

EXERCISE E   *'It should be noted that'*

Another type of impersonal construction has the pattern *It* + passive verb + *that*. Rewrite the following sentences, moving the words in brackets to the front of the sentence. Change the verb in brackets into the passive, and add *that*. For example:

The differential rates of population growth are subject to change (we should note, however).
It should be noted, however, that the differential rates of population growth are subject to change.

1. We prefer to elect representatives because a large population is unwieldy and most people are too busy to function in government except at election time (we may note).
2. A crisis involving the whole group or territory is the sort of situation out of which the idea of discipline for the whole group would arise (we can see).

3. In normal times there is a great deal of unemployment (we do not usually recognize).
4. Agriculture grew out of women's work and was presumably developed by women (we suppose).
5. The existence of towns depends in the first place on the creation of an economic surplus (we have often argued).
6. The standard of living is not a matter solely of the relation between population and food supply (we see, then).
7. The planning made possible by government control increases the efficiency of production (we may argue).
8. A combination of geographical and cultural factors determines the distribution of population at any given time (in the chapter on human ecology, we showed).

EXERCISE F   *'It is possible that', 'It is reasonable to conclude that'*

Compare the impersonal constructions:

It is possible that the city as we know it today will not exist several hundred years hence.
It is reasonable to conclude that the city as we know it today will not exist several hundred years hence.

Rewrite the following sentences, moving the words in brackets to the front of the sentence, and adding *that*.

1. Among mature human beings competition generally takes place on the psychological rather than the physical level (significant).
2. In a capitalist society wealth is striven for competitively, while in a communist society it is sought after co-operatively (customary, believe).
3. A high positive correlation exists between social class position and educational and professional success (possible, demonstrate).
4. The feudal system is found among preliterate peoples in many parts of the world, including Peru, Mexico, Africa and Polynesia (important, note).
5. Death is more likely to occur in early childhood and after fifty years of age than at other times (apparent from the table).
6. A small rural community will not have many specialized shops or places of entertainment (obvious).
7. During the million or so years when man was evolving, his economic life centred almost exclusively on food (practically certain).
8. The further back in time we go, the smaller the population of the world will be (reasonable, conclude).

EXERCISE G   *Writing paragraphs based on census data*

1. Use the information in Figure 4(a) to complete the paragraph below.

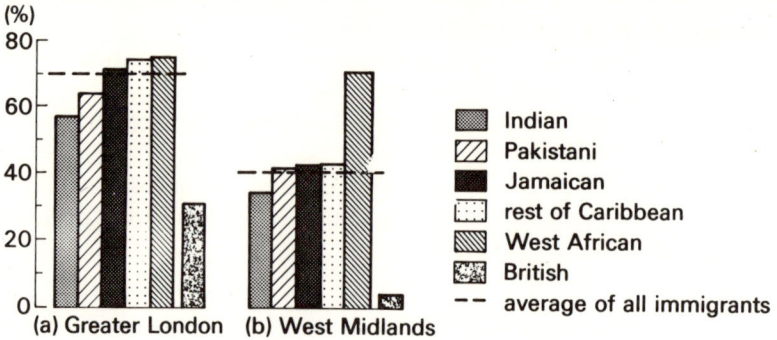

FIGURE 4   *Shared households in Greater London and the West Midlands. Data from the 1966 census.*

Figure 4(a) shows the percentage of shared households in Greater London. About 58% of immigrants from . . . shared accommodation in 1966. About . . . of Pakistani immigrants did so. Over 70% of immigrants from . . . and the rest . . . were in shared households. Some . . . of British people shared accommodation. The average percentage of all immigrants living in shared households in Greater London in 1966 was . . . . Therefore the percentage of immigrants in shared housing was more than . . . as large as that of the native population.

2. Use the information in Figure 4(b) to write a paragraph, similar to the one above, on shared households in the West Midlands.

3. Refer to Figure 4 and complete the following:
   The shortage of housing in the London area can be shown by comparing the two tables in Figure 4. In Greater London some . . . of the immigrant population shared accommodation. In the West Midlands the average was . . . . Therefore some . . . more of the immigrants resident in London shared . . . than did those resident in . . . . The tables show that 58% of . . . in London shared compared with . . . in the West Midlands, or about . . . more. Of the Pakistani immigrants . . . more shared housing in . . . than did in . . . . People from Jamaica and the rest of the Caribbean showed a similar difference, i.e. about . . . and . . . more respectively. However, some . . . of West African immigrants shared accommodation in . . . compared with . . . in . . . . This is a difference of only . . . .

4. Write two paragraphs on households sharing kitchens, using the information in Figure 5. The first paragraph should describe the situation in Greater London, and the second the situation in the West Midlands. Use paragraphs 1 and 2 as a guide.

(%)
40
20
0
(a) Greater London
(b) West Midlands
Indian
Pakistani
Jamaican
rest of Caribbean
West African
British
average of all immigrants

FIGURE 5 *Households sharing kitchens in Greater London and the West Midlands. Data from the 1966 census.*

5. Using paragraph 3 as a guide, and with reference to Figure 5, write a comparison of the situation in Greater London and the West Midlands with respect to households sharing kitchens. Begin your comparison as follows:

   Although 30% more of the immigrant population shared accommodation in the London area than in the West Midlands, there was little difference in the percentage of immigrant households sharing a kitchen.

III GUIDED WRITING

EXERCISE H

Study the following notes for a paragraph on European migration to the United States. The notes are arranged in nine groups, and each group corresponds to a sentence in the paragraph. Join each group of notes into one sentence, using the additional material in brackets. Make any other changes that you think are necessary. Be careful about articles, tenses and punctuation.

1. America – large numbers of migrants from Europe – economic opportunity – religious, civil liberty (attracted, because, offered).
2. Voyages of primitive Polynesians remarkable – twelfth-century Vikings used boats – took them from Scandinavia to North America, Constantinople – no great redistribution of population possible – development of large steamships (although, and, which, until, in modern times).
3. Consider history of migration over long period of time – several factors – influence movement of people from one country to another (when we, it is apparent that, there are, which).
4. Impetus – potato famine, Ireland – Huguenots, a religious group, oppressed in France – revolution in Germany (was provided, such situations as, the . . . of).
5. One factor – is transport available? (the . . . of . . .).

6. All these factors – many Europeans migrated – more than 30,000,000 in less than a century (as a result of, combined, to the United States, going).
7. Another factor – causes people to migrate – unfavourable conditions at home.
8. Nineteenth century – new land in United States – until 1882 free movement in and out of country (during, abundant supply, no restriction).
9. Other factors – new land available? – restrictions on mobility absent? (significant, include).

EXERCISE I

Check that you have nine good sentences. Make sure you know all the words, using a dictionary if necessary. Rearrange the sentences so that they combine to make a logical paragraph. Write a final version of the entire paragraph.

IV   READING AND NOTE-TAKING

EXERCISE J   *Priming questions*

Read the following passage quickly to get a general idea of its contents. Find and write out the answers to the following questions:

1. What is an in-group?
2. What is acculturation?
3. Why were the Protestants persecuted in seventeenth-century France?

Society in general can be defined as a large group of people with certain identifiable characteristics, such as a common language, who have over a period of time worked out a way of life together. The members of a society accept definite patterns of employment, distribution of goods, marriage and procreation, and entertainment. They share certain norms, moral standards, and expectations. Because they wish to survive as a group, they organize the educational process to ensure that children learn the accepted standards of their society. Furthermore, they set up authorities to guar-antee the continuation of these standards. And, of course, they react against pressures for change whether they originate within the society through a younger generation or come from an outside group.

Social minorities share a set of cultural assumptions, methods and goals which may differ in certain respects from those of the larger group. Most importantly a minority tends to see itself as an in-group, and often because of fear its members feel antagonism towards the out-group. In such a climate small inoffensive acts on the part of the minority may be seen as aggressive by the majority, and vice versa. Thus, social tensions are common in situations of social plurality. Groups which do not wish to integrate, however, may welcome a certain degree of tension because it has the effect of drawing the members of the group together. For example, during periods of persecution Jews have retained a strong sense of group identity, but in more tolerant times Jewish customs and religious practices have tended to decrease and marriages with members of the majority group have become more common.

Generally speaking, there are two ways in which the members of a society may try to solve the problems posed by the presence of a minority group. They may try to eliminate the minority altogether, or they may decide to tolerate it. The elimination of minorities may take the form of assimilation, suppression or ejection. Assimilation (sometimes called acculturation) is found when groups of individuals having different cultures come into continuous first-hand contact, with subsequent changes in the original cultural patterns of either or both groups. An example of successful assimilation is provided by the United States in the nineteenth and early twentieth centuries. During this period large groups of immigrants and their children, many of them speaking foreign languages, were assimilated very rapidly as a result of education and cultural indoctrination. The contrasting method, that of ejecting an unacceptable minority or suppressing those who remain, has been resorted to many times in many parts of the world. A striking example is found in seventeenth-century France, when Protestants were banished or driven into concealment if they refused to change their religion. A minority may be tolerated even if it is not popular. This may happen if the aims and organization of the minority are not felt to be sufficiently objectionable to justify elimination, or if the majority believes it to be morally wrong to assimilate, suppress or eject the minority.

The toleration of ethnic and cultural minority groups can produce a wide range of different types of social organization. In extreme cases a minority may be completely segregated, as in the case of the Jews in medieval Europe. Alternatively, separation can be achieved by discrimination of various degrees of intensity, which typically involves excluding the minority group from goods and privileges valued by members of the society.

EXERCISE K   *Notes*

Now read the passage more slowly and carefully and think about the main point or points in each paragraph.

Below there are eight statements based on the passage. Write out the statements in the correct order so that they summarize the most important points in each paragraph. Arrange your notes in four sections to correspond to the four paragraphs. Within each section, make the relationship between the statements clear by using the logical connectors *furthermore, however, on the one hand, on the other hand, in some cases, alternatively.*

1. A minority may be eliminated by assimilating it into the majority group, or by suppressing it.
2. A society which contains minorities may experience certain tensions.
3. A minority may be tolerated, if elimination is felt to be unjustified, or morally wrong.
4. Toleration may result in the complete segregation of the minority.
5. These tensions may be welcomed by some, since they have the effect of drawing the members of a minority group together.
6. As members of a society we share certain norms, moral standards and expectations.
7. The separation of minorities can be brought about by various types of discrimination.
8. We seek to preserve our social standards by setting up authorities and organizing the educational process.

DISCUSSION

What is the attitude to social minorities in your own country?

7 Urbanization

I READING AND COMPREHENSION

[1]It is generally agreed that the first true cities appeared about 5000 years ago in the food-producing communities of the Middle East. [2]The cities of Sumeria, Egypt and the Indus Valley possessed a number of characteristics which distinguished them as truly urban. [3]The cities were very much larger and more densely populated than any previous settlement, and their function was clearly differentiated from that of the surrounding villages. [4]In the cities the old patterns of kinship relations were replaced by a complex hierarchy of social classes based on the specialization of labour. [5]The cities acquired the basis for an effective capital by collecting the surplus of the primary producers in the villages. [6]Moreover, the need to keep records led to the development of writing and arithmetic, and the increased sophistication of urban society gave a new impetus to artistic expression of every kind.

[7]When the basis of city life was established in Europe the urban tradition was drawn from the ancient cities of the Middle East, via the civilizations of Greece and Rome. [8]We can trace three main phases in the growth of the West European city. [9]The first of these is the medieval phase, which extends from the beginning of the eleventh century A.D. to about 1500. [10]The second is the Renaissance and Baroque phase which can be traced from about 1500 to the beginning of the nineteenth century. [11]The third is the modern phase, extending from the early nineteenth century to the present day.

(a) *The origins of the urban tradition in Europe are to be found in the cities of Greece and Rome.*

(b) *The Renaissance and Baroque phase of European urban development lasted for about three hundred years.*

[12]Every medieval city began as a small settlement which grew up round a geographical or cultural focal point. [13]This would often be a permanent structure such as a stronghold, a cathedral or a large church. [14]In districts where travel and trade were well established, it might be a market, a river crossing, or a place where two or more trade routes converged. [15]In studies of urban geography the oldest part of a town is referred to as the nuclear settlement. [16]There are many small towns in Europe where it is still possible to trace the outline of the original nuclear settlement. [17]It is, of course, much

more difficult to do this in the case of a large modern city which has grown to many times its original size.

[18]From the point of view of the urban geographer, a city is essentially a group of dwellings arranged in such a way that the inhabitants can share in a variety of co-operative enterprises. [19]All urban settlements must meet a number of basic requirements. [20]They must be reasonably compact in form, so that all parts of the town are easily accessible. [21]There must be adequate space between the buildings for pedestrian or vehicular traffic, and special areas or buildings must be set aside for public functions. [22]Perhaps most important of all, the citizens must have security to enable them to carry on their affairs. [23]For this reason the earliest settlements were often attached to an existing castle. [24]At a later stage, when urban settlements were larger and more prosperous, the citizens usually surrounded the towns with walls of their own. [25]Towns founded in the later Middle Ages were almost invariably surrounded by a strong wall. [26]Each town had become, in effect, a fortress in itself.

(c)   *It can be assumed that every medieval city began as a settlement based on a market.*

(d)   *Security has always been a vital consideration in the development of urban communities.*

[27]The decision to establish a settlement in a particular place depended basically on two factors, politico-cultural and economic. [28]The builders of a fortress or important church were motivated primarily by politico-cultural considerations. [29]These builders sought a prominent hill site or a promontory surrounded on three sides by sea, river or marsh. [30]Such a site dominated the surrounding countryside and had the benefit of natural defences. [31]On the other hand, an economic community required, above all, easy access, room to expand, and contact with the main trade routes. [32]For this reason, a particularly favoured urban site was on fairly flat land by a navigable waterway. [33]The two primary functions, politico-cultural and economic, were often combined in a single settlement which included both a hilltop and low-lying ground. [34]Thus, in the old Greek cities the Acropolis lay on the hilltop and the town on the lower slopes. [35]In France and Belgium we find the same combination of the Haute-Ville and the Basse-Ville, which in Germany are called the Oberstadt and the Unterstadt. [36]In each case the cathedral or secular stronghold, or both, is situated on a hill, and the main part of the urban community is in the valley below.

[37]There was a tendency in the Middle Ages for the same ideas to be repeated again and again in the establishment of different towns. [38]As a result we can distinguish not only certain recurring systems of urban planning, but also families of towns which have the same basic features of design.

(e)   *Politico-cultural and economic factors were both important in selecting a site for a medieval town.*

(f) *The ancient Greek settlements had certain points in common with the cities of medieval Europe.*

SOLUTIONS

Complete the following statements by referring to the passage above.

(a) Although the . . . in Europe is based partly on the . . . of Greece and Rome, the first . . . appeared earlier in Sumeria, Egypt and the Indus Valley.

i.e. The origins of the urban tradition in Europe are not to be found in the cities of Greece and Rome, but in the earlier communities of the Middle East.

(b) The Renaissance and Baroque period represents the . . . in the growth of the West European city. This phase continued from . . . to the beginning of the . . . , or about the year 1800.

i.e. *The Renaissance and Baroque phase of European urban development lasted for about three hundred years.*

(c) All medieval cities grew up round a geographic or cultural . . . . This might be, for example, . . . , . . . or . . . .

∴ It cannot be assumed that every medieval city began as a settlement based on a market.

(d) The first settlements were often attached to . . . . When cities became larger and more prosperous, they were usually surrounded by . . . . The . . . could not have carried on their affairs without a reasonable measure of . . . .

i.e. *Security has always been a vital consideration in the development of urban communities.*

(e) The two primary functions of a medieval town were . . . . Where . . . factors were the main consideration, the town tended to be built on a hill or an easily . . . promontory. An . . . community, on the other hand, was more likely to be . . . on flat land by a navigable waterway.

i.e. *Politico-cultural and economic factors were both important in selecting a site for a medieval town.*

(f) 'Families' of towns are towns which have the same basic . . . . In many French, Belgian and German towns the . . . is on a hill and the . . . lies in the valley below. The same . . . can be found in the old Greek cities.

∴ *The ancient Greek settlements had certain points in common with the cities of medieval Europe.*

EXERCISE A   *Meaning assessment and summary writing*

1. Refer to the passage and decide whether the following statements are true or false.

(a) The growth of cities made possible the development of a hierarchy of professional classes.

(b) The need for security led to improved methods of urban defence.

(c) The urban communities of Sumeria, Egypt and the Indus Valley were different in every way from the great cities of today.

(d) The increased sophistication of urban society led to new heights of artistic achievement.

(e) The urban revolution which began 5000 years ago was profoundly significant from the social, the economic, the cultural and the military points of view.

(f) Medieval towns were invariably built on a prominent hill site which dominated the surrounding countryside and had the benefit of natural defence.

(g) The growth of cities resulted in the accumulation of capital and led to the development of trade and commerce.

(h) The growth of cities often led to a revival of the old patterns of kinship relations.

2. What contribution has the city made to human civilization? Write an answer to this question, using the true statements above but arranging them differently. Write a paragraph containing five sentences, with additional material as follows:

(a) . . .

(b) It was socially significant because . . .

(c) It was . . .

(d) It was . . .

(e) Finally, . . .

EXERCISE B   *Contextual reference*

Refer to the context in which the following sentences appear and replace or expand the expressions printed in italics so as to make the meaning clear.

1. The first *of these* is the medieval phase, which extends from the beginning of the eleventh century A.D. to about 1500. (9)

2. In districts where travel and trade were well established, *it* might be a market, a river crossing or a place where two or more trade routes converged. (14)

3. It is much more difficult *to do this* in the case of a large modern city which has grown to many times its original size. (17)

4. *Such a site* dominated the surrounding countryside and had the benefit of natural defences. (30)

5. *For this reason*, a particularly favoured urban site was on fairly flat land by a navigable waterway. (32)

6. *As a result*, we can distinguish not only certain recurring systems of urban planning, but also families of towns which have the same basic features of design. (38)

EXERCISE C   *Relationships between statements*

Link the following statements together to form a paragraph using the logical connectors given below. The statements are already in the right order.

   although, sometimes, in other cases, thus, however

1. A modern city has been defined as a settlement with a population of more than 200,000.
2. For statistical purposes this is as convenient a criterion as any.
3. It is clear that the concepts of 'village', 'town', and 'city' cannot be fully defined in terms of numbers alone.
4. There are circumstances in which a numerically small community has urban characteristics, such as density of population and administrative functions.
5. We may find a settlement which is numerically large, but is still obviously a village with the majority of inhabitants employed as farmers.
6. Density of population and function may be better criteria for determining where the line should be drawn between a large village and a small town.
7. In India a town is officially defined as a settlement with a population of more than 5000, with a density of over 1000 people to the square mile, and with over 75% of the adult male population engaged in non-agricultural work.
8. India appears to be exceptional in placing so much emphasis on density of population.
9. In most countries function rather than density is regarded as the critical factor.

II   USE OF LANGUAGE

EXERCISE D   *Nouns formed from verbs*

In English we often find nouns which have been formed from verbs. Look at the following examples:

imitate	→	imitation
grow	→	growth
inherit	→	inheritance
restrain	→	restraint
develop	→	development

Combine each of the pairs of sentences below into a single sentence. The words in italics should be replaced by nouns formed from verbs. For example:

People *accumulate* private property. Among the Zuni there is no emphasis on *this process*.

Among the Zuni there is no emphasis on the accumulation of private property.

1. The function of maintaining order in a given territory *was developed.* The origin of the state lies in this process.
2. Economic activities *are regulated.* This is not new, but is as old as economic organization itself.
3. People *dispose* of their property at death. This reflects social attitudes towards property.
4. Social structures *are important.* This can be seen in what functions they perform.
5. Mechanical sources of power *were applied* to production. This took place first in the field of handicrafts.
6. We usually *conceive* of a city as follows. It is a place where people do not raise the food they eat but make something which they can exchange for food.
7. The inhabitants *identify* with their locality. Even where people continue to live in small communities, this may be lessened by modern communications and transport.
8. Population *is distributed* by geographic regions. This is affected by climate, how good the earth's surface may be, where natural resources are, and whether there are any waterways.

EXERCISE E   *Stating a consequence or result*

A consequence or result may be stated in several ways:

(a) Bantu culture puts a great premium on oratory, *so* nearly all the men are fluent in their speech.
(b) Bantu culture puts a great premium on oratory; *as a result*, nearly all the men are fluent in their speech.
(c) Bantu culture puts a great premium on oratory; *consequently* nearly all the men are fluent in their speech.

All the above could be written as two sentences. It is unusual to begin a sentence with 'so' except in informal contexts. We can begin a sentence with 'as a result' or 'consequently' in formal or informal contexts. Combine each of the following, using 'so', 'consequently' or 'as a result'. In each case, decide whether to use one sentence or two, and punctuate appropriately.

1. In modern society scientific enquiry is viewed with great favour. An outstanding figure like Einstein may become something of a national celebrity.
2. The members of a group disapprove of individuals who deviate too far from approved patterns. Individuals do not as a rule rise much above, or fall far below, the average level of the group.

3. An audience is different from a crowd. In an audience, attention is focused primarily upon some outside activity. The members are not greatly affected by one another's presence or behaviour.

4. The reduction in the death rate has been most marked in the case of infants. The lives of infants are saved, which has the same effect as increasing the birthrate.

5. The early primitive communities were self-sufficient economically. They did not depend upon trade.

6. Unemployment is sometimes due to world depression or to the rapid introduction of new machinery. It is not wholly caused by the *laissez-faire* features of our economic system.

7. A heterogeneous society contains many different groups. These groups differ in terms of education, attitudes and social backgrounds. It is easy to find misunderstanding among them and difficult to find agreement.

8. Modern research shows that the personality of the child is, to a large extent, dependent upon the way the early years are spent. The responsibility placed on the parents is very great.

EXERCISE F   *Making explanations*

We can make an explanation in several different ways:

(a) Primary groups are effective *because* they are personal in nature.

(b) $\left. \begin{array}{l} \textit{Because} \\ \textit{Since} \end{array} \right\}$ they are personal in nature, primary groups are effective.

(c) Primary groups are personal in nature, *and for this reason* they are effective.

Combine each of the following into a single sentence, using 'because', 'since' or 'for this reason'. The sentences you write should make sense. You may use any one of the above patterns, but remember that there are often reasons for preferring one pattern rather than another.

1. An individual does not feel ridiculous when he gestures and shouts at a football match. Others are doing the same, and so his behaviour is not conspicuous.

2. Individuals live in groups. The behaviour of each individual is affected by the behaviour of others.

3. The identification of individuals with one another is greater in primary groups. The effects on personality are greater.

4. Class membership, once obtained, is socially inherited. Upper-class position is often retained by families which once had wealth but have it no more.

5. The sociologist is interested in the question of mental disorders. Such disorders have many social implications.

6. There is no end to the things that people want and that money can supply. There is a danger that the hunger for money can become insatiable.

7. Members of a minority group differ from members of the majority group in appearance, habits and attitudes. Prejudice develops towards them and they are discriminated against.
8. Galileo was persecuted. His teaching deviated too far from the general beliefs of his time.

EXERCISE G   *Paragraph writing based on historical diagrams*

1. Study the following key.

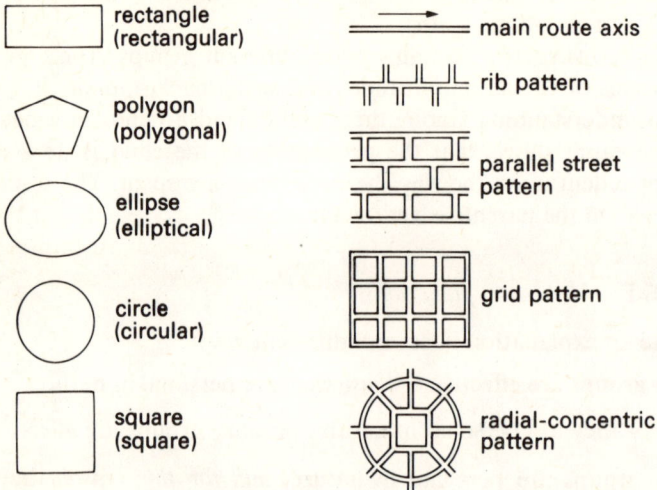

rectangle (rectangular)

polygon (polygonal)

ellipse (elliptical)

circle (circular)

square (square)

main route axis

rib pattern

parallel street pattern

grid pattern

radial-concentric pattern

2. Read the following description, and compare it with the diagram.

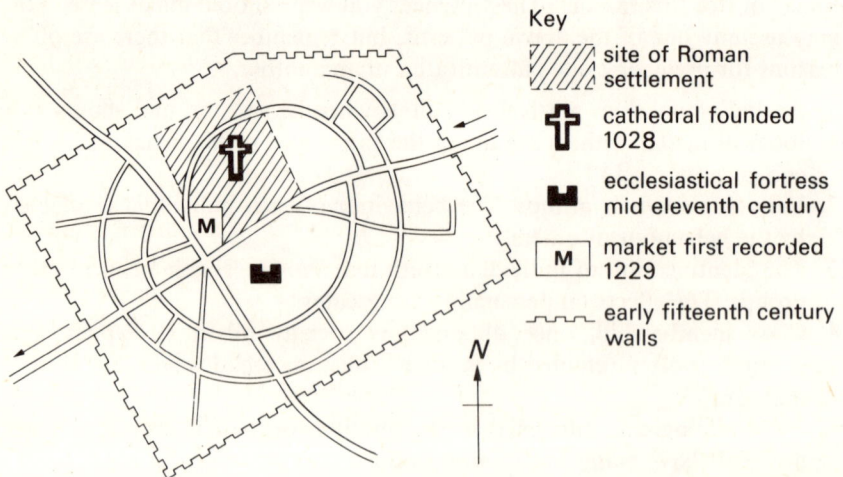

Key

site of Roman settlement

cathedral founded 1028

ecclesiastical fortress mid eleventh century

market first recorded 1229

early fifteenth century walls

N

Town A

Town A grew up on the site of a Roman settlement on a main route axis running from the north-east to the south-west. The nucleus of settlement was a cathedral founded in 1028 and an ecclesiastical fortress built in the mid eleventh century. A market, south-west of the cathedral, was first recorded in 1229. The walls were built in the early fifteenth century in the form of an irregular polygon. Further growth tended to radiate outwards from the cathedral and market place, thus forming an example of the 'radical-concentric' type of urban development.

3. Draw a diagram, with a key, to illustrate each of the following descriptions.

(a) Town B grew up on a main route axis running from the south-east to the north-west. The nucleus of settlement was a tenth century fortress and a church founded in 998. A market, north of the main east-west axis and located between the fortress and the church was first recorded in 1156. The walls were built in the thirteenth century roughly in the form of a square. Further growth proceeded at right angles to the main axis to form what may be called the 'rib pattern' type of urban development.

(b) Town C grew up at the confluence of two rivers on a main route axis running from north to south. The nucleus of settlement was a cathedral founded in 1071. A fortress was built at the end of the eleventh century on the site of the Roman settement, and a market, immediately to the south of the cathedral, was first recorded in 1306. The university was founded in 1390. The walls were built in the fourteenth century to a roughly polygonal plan. Further growth included two secondary thoroughfares running parallel to the main axis, with transverse streets interconnecting to form the 'parallel street' pattern of urban development.

(c) Town D grew up on a main east–west axis running from Coblenz to Luneburg. The settlement was located on a promontory surrounded by marshes on three sides, and the nucleus of settlement was a twelfth century fortress and a church founded in 1162. A market, to the north-east of the church, had been established by 1336. The fourteenth century walls form an almost perfect rectangle. The streets are based on a rectilinear plan and are spaced at more or less equal intervals. The town is a good example of the 'grid pattern' type of urban development.

4. Write paragraphs based on the following diagrams.

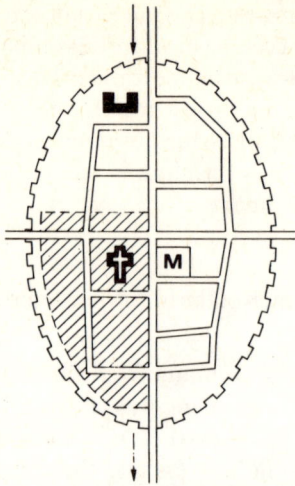

Key

///// site of Roman settlement

⊔ fortress mid eleventh century

✝ cathedral church founded 1067

M market first recorded 1246

⌐⌐ early fourteenth century walls

N ↑

(a) *Town E*

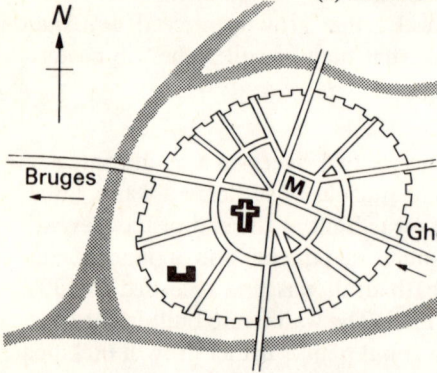

N ↑

Bruges ←

Ghent

Key

✝ cathedral founded 1023

⊔ ecclesiastical fortress early twelfth century

M market first recorded 1298

⌐⌐ late thirteenth century walls

(b) *Town F*

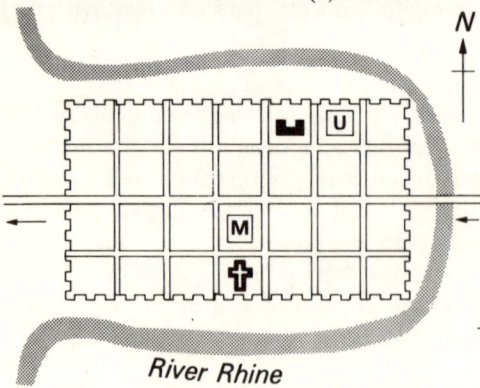

N ↑

Key

✝ cathedral founded 996

⊔ fortress early eleventh century

M market first recorded 1316

U university founded 1409

⌐⌐ fifteenth century walls

River Rhine

III GUIDED WRITING

EXERCISE H

Study the following notes for a paragraph on Renaissance town planning. The notes are arranged in nine groups, and each group corresponds to a sentence in the paragraph. Join each group of notes into one sentence, using the additional material in brackets. Make any other changes that you think are necessary. Be careful about articles, tenses and punctuation.

1. Destruction walls Constantinople Turkish artillery 1453 – necessary important towns in strategic locations – surrounded by elaborate fortifications – cannon could be mounted – fired at attacking forces (after, it became, to be, on which, to be).
2. Another factor in Renaissance town planning – not previously known in acute form – use of horses, horse-drawn carriages (which, such an, increasing).
3. One factor – emerged late fifteenth century – construct fortifications – resist iron cannon balls – propelled by gunpowder (which, need to, capable of).
4. Renaissance towns – influenced by several factors – unknown in ancient times (the building of, which, virtually).
5. Close relationship – landscape, town planning – eighteenth century urban planning – seventeenth century formal gardens (developed between, and, strongly influenced by).
6. Model for early formal garden planning – Pierro Ligorio's creation at Villa d'Este – Tivoli in Italy – broad plains of France – seventeenth century parks constructed on grandest scale (although, near, it was on, that).
7. Gradual change in scale of cities – wider, straighter streets – facilitate movement (gave rise to, resulting in).
8. Fortification systems extremely expensive – proved rigid barrier to later urban expansion – maximum use made – land in middle of towns (such, and, so that, building).
9. A third factor – new fashion – formal gardens – serve as setting – symmetrical architecture – large houses.

EXERCISE I

Check that you have nine good sentences. Make sure you know all the words, using a dictionary if necessary. Rearrange the sentences so that they combine to make a logical paragraph. Write a final version of the entire paragraph.

IV READING AND NOTE-TAKING

EXERCISE J *Priming questions*

Read the following passage quickly to get a general idea of the contents. Find and write out the answers to the following questions:

1. What proportion of the world's population live in towns?
2. What is a metropolis?
3. Is it possible for a city to get too big?

Although some cities grew greatly in size during the Renaissance period, the metropolitan city as we know it today has its roots in the industrial revolution. Up to that time the process of urbanization had affected only a small minority of the population. From the beginning of the nineteenth century, however, three major economic factors led to the growth of cities on an entirely new scale. Firstly, the invention of powerful new machines gave rise to factories of unprecedented size, which created an enormous demand for labour. Secondly, the large-scale construction of roads, railways and canals provided cheap and regular transport which made possible the concentration of industries and population into particular areas. Thirdly, a revolution in agriculture led to the development of an efficient system of mixed farming, new methods of breeding and an increase in the yield of corn, all of which helped to provide the food necessary to sustain a greatly increased urban population.

The process of urban growth is still closely linked to industrial development, but the increased complexity of administration and commerce has also contributed to the rapid rate of urbanization. It has been estimated that in 1800 less than 3% of the population of the world, or 27·4 million people, lived in towns of over 5000 inhabitants. By 1950 the proportion of town-dwellers had grown to nearly 30%, or over 716 million. Moreover, during the last half-century, it is the large city which has succeeded in attracting population to a much greater degree than small cities or towns.

The typical modern metropolis has been described as a concentration of at least 500,000 people living within an area in which the travelling time from the outskirts to the centre is about 40 minutes. The metropolis has four major components: a central business complex; a collection of manufacturing and allied industries; a quantity of housing with its attendant services; and an area of open land. The central business complex is made up of diversified retail businesses, financial institutions and offices of the public administration. A generation ago it was usual to find factories competing with business premises for space in the central area, but the present tendency is for manufacturing industries to move to the outskirts of the city where land is cheaper. Housing accounts for the largest amount of occupied land in the metropolis, and also presents the greatest problems in the form of slums, or sub-standard dwellings, and the segregation of people by income or race. The fourth major component of the metropolis – open land maintained for recreational use – is currently of great concern to urban planners.

It has been claimed that with the development of the modern metropolis the city has undergone a qualitative change. It is no longer merely a larger version of the traditional city, but an entirely new form of settlement. Moreover, it is a form which may contain within itself the seeds of its own decay. What are the arguments that have been used by the critics of the modern super-city? Some critics object that a great modern metropolis can exist only if it is parasitic upon the surrounding countryside, thus draining it of its economic and social strength. Another accusation against the metropolis is that it has been instrumental in dissolving the system of social ties that exist in small communities, thus helping to produce an 'ant heap' form of society that lacks values and standards of behaviour. Perhaps there is more substance in the argument that the modern metropolis will eventually be choked to death by its own growth. It is possible to find indications of this trend in the gross overcrowding of Calcutta or the proliferation of motorways in Los Angeles. Certainly, an indispensable requirement of the future will be careful planning with the aim of achieving a rational distribution of the urban population, and of their various activities. Another requirement will be the development of cheap and efficient public transport facilities to connect the various parts of the metropolis.

EXERCISE K *Notes*

Now read the passage more slowly and carefully and think about the main points in each paragraph. Make notes as follows:

1. State three factors which led to the growth of big cities during the nineteenth century.
2. State three reasons why big cities are continuing to grow.
3. State the four components of a typical modern metropolis.
4. State three criticisms that have been made of the modern metropolis.
5. State two things that can be done to alleviate the present problems.

DISCUSSION

Is it inevitable that cities should continue to grow bigger and bigger?

8 The problem of traffic in towns

I READING AND COMPREHENSION

[1]In 1961 the Government of the United Kingdom set up a study group led by Colin Buchanan to enquire into the long-term development of roads and traffic in urban areas and their influence on the urban environment. [2]One result of the enquiry was the publication of *Traffic in Towns*.* [3]This volume, known as 'The Buchanan Report', was the first attempt at a comprehensive treatment of the problem. [4]The following paragraphs summarize some of the main points from the introduction to the report.

[5]The motor vehicle is, basically, a beneficial invention with an enormous potential demand for its services. [6]At the same time it has to be admitted that traffic congestion resulting from the widespread use of cars has adversely affected the lives of many millions of people. [7]The difficulties arising from the increasing use of motor vehicles are of two distinct kinds.

[8]First we must consider the adverse effect of crowded roads on the efficiency of the motor vehicle itself. [9]Congestion is brought about not only by the multiplication of vehicles on the roads but also by the inadequacies of the inherited urban road system. [10]Congestion is also caused by the fact that access to the majority of buildings is gained direct from the street, with the result that the traffic flow is obstructed every time a vehicle pulls up to deliver callers or goods. [11]A further difficulty is the shortage of suitable places for parking, so that finding somewhere to stop is now a major anxiety attendant upon every urban journey by car.

(a) *On the whole the invention of the motor car has brought more advantages than disadvantages.*

(b) *Cars are likely to become increasingly efficient under present conditions.*

[12]In addition to the frustration of drivers we must consider the many undesirable by-products of the use of motor vehicles. [13]These fall into two main categories: accidents, and the deterioration of the environment.

[14]It can be shown that the number of accidents on the roads is not proportional to the total number of vehicles in circulation. [15]For example, a fourfold increase between 1934 and 1960 in the number of vehicles in use in

* London: Her Majesty's Stationery Office, 1963.

Britain led only to a 45% increase in casualties. [16]The reasons for this are various and no doubt include better vehicle design, the elimination of 'black spots' on the roads and a gradual improvement in standards of behaviour on the part of both drivers and pedestrians. [17]Nevertheless, in Britain in 1961 accidents involving motor vehicles accounted for nearly one-third of all fatalities, and must therefore be regarded as a very great social evil.

[18]The deterioration of the environment due to the increasing use of motor vehicles can be divided into a number of different aspects. [19]Four of the most important can be considered under the headings of safety, noise, fumes and visual intrusion. [20]The increasingly hazardous nature of the urban environment affects everyone, not only those who are unfortunate enough to be involved in road accidents.

(c) *As the number of vehicles increases, it can be assumed that the number of accidents will increase proportionately.*
(d) *It is reasonable to assume that high standards of vehicle design will always be a factor contributing to road safety.*

[21]In addition to danger and anxiety, the motor vehicle is responsible for a great deal of noise. [22]In 1963 an official committee set up by the Minister for Science reported that traffic noise is now the predominant nuisance in towns, and that noise levels were capable of being much reduced. [23]Another unpleasant by-product of the motor vehicle is fumes and smell. [24]In Britain, engine fumes do not yet rank as a major cause of atmospheric pollution as they do in California, but there is no doubt that fumes are rendering urban streets extremely unpleasant, and that the nuisance is becoming all-pervasive. [25]Finally, we must consider the visual consequences of the transport revolution. [26]These include the destruction of many areas valued for their architectural beauty or historical associations, and the construction of roads and bridges which are often violently out of scale with their surroundings.

[27]The problem of traffic in towns is a problem of design. [28]In order to provide for the needs of both drivers and pedestrians we must redesign the physical arrangement of streets and buildings which we have inherited from the past. [29]This must be done in such a way as to allow the efficient distribution of traffic while preserving a satisfactory standard of environment. [30]In examining the traffic problem in any specific area, we have to weigh three considerations against one another. What standard of environment do we require? To what extent are we prepared to allow environmental arguments to interfere with our freedom of movement as motorists? [31]Finally, if we wish to reconcile the competing demands of traffic and environment, how much money are we prepared to spend on physical alterations?

(e) *Traffic noise is a serious nuisance, but it is less serious than the fumes and smell produced by motor vehicles.*
(f) *In replanning our towns, environmental considerations must take precedence over the needs of the motorist.*

SOLUTIONS

(a) One can point to many . . . arising from the increasing use of motor vehicles. However, the motor vehicle is basically a . . . invention. In spite of . . . roads and the shortage of suitable places for . . . there is an enormous . . . demand for its services.

∴ *Judging by the demand for car ownership, the invention of the motor car must have brought more advantages than disadvantages.*

(b) The inadequacies of the . . . road system have an . . . effect on the efficiency of the motor vehicle. In other words, cars tend to be . . . under present conditions. As the number of vehicles on the roads multiplies, . . . on the roads is likely to get worse.

i.e. Cars are likely to become increasingly inefficient under present conditions.

(c) Between 1934 and 1960 the number of . . . in use in Britain was multiplied by four (= increased . . .). However, it can be shown that the number of . . . increased by only . . . over the same period.

∴ It cannot be assumed that as the number of vehicles increases, the number of accidents will increase proportionately.

(d) We have seen that there was a . . . decrease in the number of road . . . between 1934 and 1960. This has been attributed partly to an . . . in the design of motor vehicles.

i.e. *It is reasonable to assume that high standards of vehicle design will always be a factor contributing to road safety.*

(e) The . . . and . . . of motor vehicles are both very unpleasant. However, in 1963 an official committee . . . that traffic noise is the . . . nuisance (i.e. the main nuisance) in towns.

i.e. Traffic noise is more serious than the fumes and smell produced by motor vehicles.

(f) In examining the . . . problem we have to . . . three considerations against one another. These are: the needs of the . . . , the needs of the . . . , and how much money is available for . . . .

i.e. In replanning our towns, neither environmental considerations nor the needs of the motorist take precedence. The aim is to reconcile the two.

EXERCISE A   *Meaning assessment and summary writing*

1. Refer to the passage and decide whether the following statements are true or false.
   (a) The factors contributing to traffic congestion include poor road design, badly planned access to buildings, and the fact that there is often nowhere suitable to park.
   (b) If we wish we can invest money in redesigning the relationship between streets and buildings.
   (c) Except at the rush hour, it is still not too difficult to find a place to park.

(d) It is widely recognized that traffic congestion in towns is causing increasingly serious problems.

(e) As time goes on, fewer and fewer people are likely to want to own a car.

(f) People are concerned both at the dangerous state of the roads, and at the general deterioration of the environment caused by noise, fumes and visual intrusion.

(g) It is far from easy to reconcile the competing demands of traffic and environment.

(h) So far the British Government has made little or no attempt to enquire into the problem of traffic in towns.

(i) A policy aimed at redesigning our inherited urban street pattern inevitably presents many difficulties.

(j) There is still hope that something can be done about the problem of traffic in towns.

(k) In California engine fumes do not yet rank as a major cause of atmospheric pollution.

(l) Traffic congestion is brought about partly by the increasing number of vehicles on the roads.

2. Can anything be done about the problem of traffic in towns? Write an answer to this question, using the true statements above. Write a paragraph containing eight sentences, adding logical connectors and making any other changes that may be necessary.

EXERCISE B *Contextual reference*

Refer to the context in which the following sentences appear and replace or expand the expressions printed in italics so as to make the meaning clear.

1. One result of *the enquiry* was the publication of 'Traffic in Towns'. (2)
2. A further *difficulty* is the shortage of suitable places for parking. (11)
3. *These* fall into two main categories: accidents, and the deterioration of the environment. (13)
4. The reasons for *this* are various and no doubt include better vehicle design, the elimination of 'black spots' on the roads and a gradual improvement in standards of behaviour on the part of both drivers and pedestrians. (16)
5. Four *of the most important* can be considered under the headings of safety, noise, fumes and visual intrusion. (19)
6. *This* must be done in such a way as to allow the efficient distribution of traffic while preserving a satisfactory standard of environment. (29)

EXERCISE C *Relationships between statements*

Write out the following paragraph, replacing the blanks with suitable expressions. The paragraph is a continuation of the reading passage.

[1]New and exciting possibilities are offered by a field of design . . . may be referred to as 'traffic architecture'. [2]. . . buildings and streets are thought of as two complementary . . . of the same design problem, . . . it may be . . . to combine them in ways . . . are more advantageous than the conventional street. [3]. . . , part of a town might be redeveloped with traffic at ground level, . . . the buildings on a raised 'deck' . . . they might be grouped in patterns related to, . . . not dictated by, the traffic below. [4]A point of major importance is . . . traffic architecture techniques cannot be applied piecemeal. [5]. . . obtain the full benefit of this approach it is essential . . . planners to be . . . to command the redevelopment of sizeable areas. [6]. . . gives rise to the issue of 'comprehensive redevelopment' . . . its controversial . . . of compulsory purchase, public financing . . . the pooling of ownerships. [7]. . . , unless answers to these questions are found, . . . the public accepts the . . . of comprehensive redevelopment over large areas, the opportunity . . . dealing imaginatively . . . the urban traffic problem will be lost.

II   LANGUAGE IN USE

EXERCISE D   *Stating a condition*

Look at the following sentence:

If (A) less labour is used, (B) there may be a period of unemployment.

'If (A)' states when (B) is true.

Write eight sentences with the pattern 'If (A), (B)'. Put each sentence from column A with a sentence from column B so that the complete sentence makes sense.

A	B
1. the members of a group hold decided views on a question	1. the businessman will see it as a loss of customers
2. an individual has attitudes which are opposed to those of the crowd	2. their standard of living will be lowered
3. a poor man is charged with a criminal offence	3. he is less likely to be swayed by popular emotion
4. a Zuni wishes to build a house	4. it interferes with production and the maintenance of social order
5. the inhabitants of a country use up all their raw materials	5. the effect is to encourage conformity to the group opinion
6. the populations of China, Russia and India begin to decrease	6. he must store away food in order to feed the whole village at a special ceremony

7. a low birthrate brings about a decrease in population

8. warfare is unduly prolonged

7. he often finds himself under a substantial handicap

8. it will be a reversal of a historical process which has been in operation for centuries

EXERCISE E *The present participle and the past participle as modifiers*

Apart from the simple adjectives in everyday use (*good* book, *new* car, *raw* materials) writers use a large number of modifiers made up of a verb root+ suffix. Two important classes of modifiers are as follows:

(a) *Present participle modifiers*
Modifiers formed from verbs by adding *-ing*
EXAMPLE
grow+ing → *growing*
a growing city = a city which is growing
a ruling class = a class which rules

(b) *Past participle modifiers*
Modifiers formed from verbs by using the appropriate past participle form (*learned, established, written, made*, etc.)
EXAMPLE
organize+ed → *organized*
organized religion = religion which someone has organized
prescribed rules = rules which someone has prescribed

Complete the following sentences, filling in the gaps with a present participle modifier or a past participle modifier. Form each modifier from one of the verbs in the list:

limit	establish
increase	initiate
inherit	precede
exist	celebrate
work	correspond
recognize	

1. Unfortunately . . . wealth is not distributed evenly, but accrues to some more than to others.
2. Not infrequently a(n) . . . church conveys the idea that the . . . social system is the will of God.
3. In his . . . study of American life and government, Lord Bryce took note of the fact that American social classes differed from those of his own country.
4. Today in many countries the more . . . allegiance to social class is being swallowed up in the larger wave of devotion to the nation.

5. As was suggested in the . . . chapter, social conflicts may be reconciled through a process of adjustment known as accommodation.
6. One reason for the decline in the rural population is the . . . efficiency of .agricultural production.
7. A(n) . . . cause of unemployment is the seasonal nature of many industries.
8. In the early stages a decrease in the birthrate will not necessarily be accompanied by a(n) . . . decrease in population growth.
9. Among the tribes of Northern New Guinea, the . . . men are organized into a religious brotherhood.
10. As a result of the severe depression, the unemployed in the United States totalled 13 million in 1933, or about a quarter of the . . . population.

EXERCISE F   *Referring to another author's work*

When we are writing an essay or a report we often want to include information which we have found in a book by another author. Note the following ways of referring to another author's work:

(a) *As Colin Buchanan has pointed out*, the problem of traffic in towns is a problem of design.
(b) *Following Buchanan (1963)* we can consider the deterioration of the environment under a number of different headings.
(c) The final factor is *what Buchanan calls* 'visual intrusion'.
(d) *The fact that* the problem of traffic in towns is a problem of design was *pointed out by Buchanan*.
(e) *As has been illustrated by Buchanan (1963)*, the number of accidents on the roads is not proportional to the total number of vehicles in circulation.
(f) *According to C. Buchanan*, the number of accidents on the roads is not proportional to the total number of vehicles in circulation.
(g) *Sir Colin Buchanan (1963) noted that* the difficulties arising from the increasing use of motor vehicles are of two distinct kinds.
(h) *In Buchanan's words*, 'the motor vehicle cannot simply be disinvented'.

Rewrite the following statements so as to include a reference to the authors whose names appear in brackets. Refer to the examples above and use each of the expressions printed in italics at least once. Where the date of the work is given, write the date in brackets after the name of the author. For example:

Nearly all members of organizations are preoccupied with status (C. I. Barnard 1946).
= As C. I. Barnard (1946) has pointed out, nearly all members of organizations are preoccupied with status.

1. In various groups within an organization there are differences of status, or unofficial channels of communication, which are not recognized by the formal organization (Roethlisberger and Dickson).

2. We may distinguish several different levels at which informal organization may be found (Brown 1954).

3. Many incentive schemes have failed to achieve their ends because the goal of high wages ran counter to group norms (French 1948).

4. At this point we must consider the circumstances leading to 'egoistic suicide' (Durkheim).

5. The chief distinguishing feature of a profession is the application of an intellectual technique to the ordinary business of life (Carr-Saunders and Wilson 1933).

6. Twenty per cent of the differences in measured intelligence in primary school children may be the result of environmental factors (P. E. Vernon 1958 and Sir Cyril Burt 1959).

7. The custom of joking involves 'a relation between two persons in which one is by custom permitted, and in some instances required, to tease or make fun of the other, who in turn is required to take no offence' (Radcliffe-Brown).

8. I propose to discuss six types of generalization in social science (M. Ginsberg 1947).

9. For example, we might attempt to explain social phenomena firstly in terms of individual biological needs and secondly in terms of 'derived cultural needs' (Malinowski).

10. An Australian of the Emu group in one tribe is forbidden to marry a woman of the Emu group in another tribe, although they are separated by over a hundred miles and are quite unrelated (Lowie).

EXERCISE G   *Paragraph writing based on a town planning proposal*

1. Figure 6 shows the environs of Newbury, a town in Berkshire, England. Trace or copy the figure into your notebook. Read the following paragraph and complete the figure, using the information in the paragraph, and the list of names and symbols provided.

> Newbury lies about 17 miles west of Reading at the intersection of the London–Bath road (route A4) and the Southampton–Birmingham road (A34), as shown in Figure 6. It is a medium-sized market town with a population of about 30,000, and has the usual range of activities of such a town. Hungerford is 7 miles to the west, Andover 15 miles to the south, and Basingstoke about 14 miles to the south-east. At Thatcham, a few miles to the east, there is a group of paper mills, and the atomic energy research establishments at Aldermaston and Harwell are two other employment centres which have a considerable influence on the pattern of traffic movement in the area.*

* This description is based on the Buchanan Report and does not take account of changes subsequent to 1963.

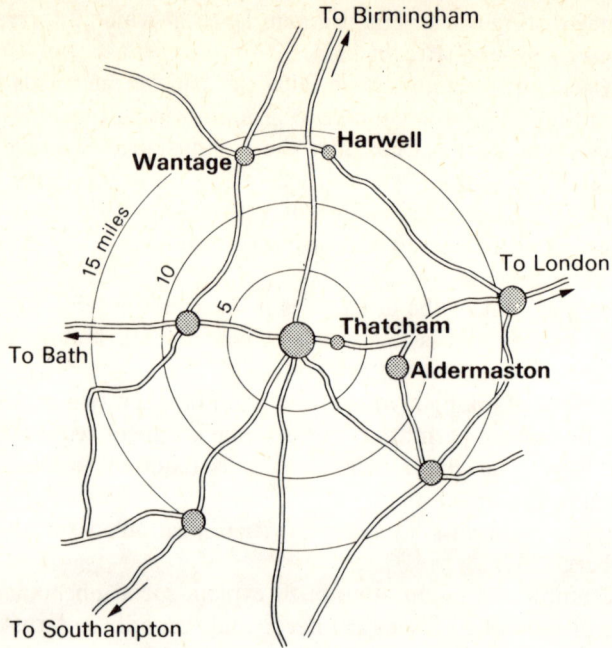

FIGURE 6   *The environs of Newbury*

Add the following names and symbols to Figure 6:
Reading	A4
Newbury	A34
Hungerford	▲▲▲ = paper mill
Andover	Ⓐ = atomic energy research establishment
Basingstoke	

2. Refer to Figure 7 and complete the following paragraph, which deals with traffic and environmental problems in the centre of Newbury.

   Figure 7 shows the central area of Newbury. This area, extending from Cheap Street in the . . . to the junction of Northbrook Street and London Road in the . . . , is of major importance from the planning point of view. This is the . . . which contains the greatest concentration of activities, and hence of . . . Northbrook Street is the principal shopping area, but there are other . . . and commercial . . . round the Market Place, and in the . . . Street, . . . and . . . area. An environmental study revealed many buildings of . . . and . . . interest, especially along Northbrook Street and round the Market Place, and extending southwards along . . . and . . . Victoria Park lies to the . . . of Park Way. The main problem in the town centre is the fact that a large volume of traffic, originating . . . and . . . of the town, is channelled through

Bartholomew Street, . . . , the Market Place and . . . , giving rise to a dangerous conflict between vehicles and pedestrians. There is a bus station . . . of the Market Place at the . . . of Park Way, and a car park on the . . . side of Wharf Road. The railway station is to the south of the town centre . . . Bartholomew Street and Cheap Street.

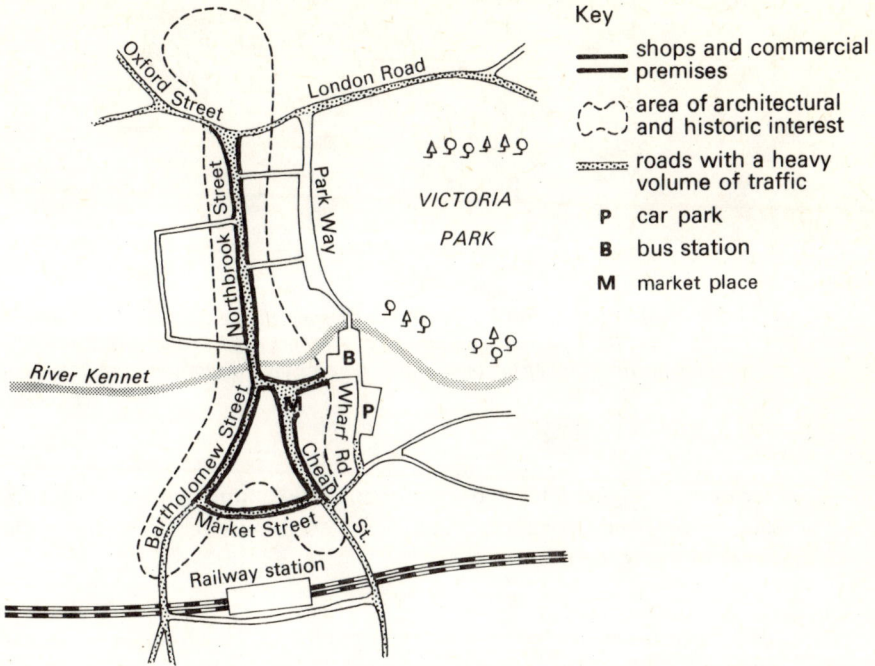

FIGURE 7   *The centre of Newbury*

3. Refer to Figure 8 and complete the following paragraph, which deals with traffic congestion due to work journeys in the Newbury and Thatcham areas.

Figure 8 shows the main zones of traffic . . . in the Newbury–Thatcham area, showing the . . . of all workers resident in each zone (R), and the percentage of all workers . . . in each zone (W). The proportion of . . . to workers contrasts sharply in the different . . . . Thus, the south zone contains 40% of . . . but only 12% of . . . , while the central zone contains . . . of workers but only . . . of residents. The north zone contains a preponderance of . . . (R 17%, W 3%), while Thatcham has a . . . of workers (. . .). The area outside the town has a . . . percentage of workers (22%) . . . residents (17%). It is clear from the diagram that . . . will contribute substantially to congestion on the roads during the . . . and evening . . . .

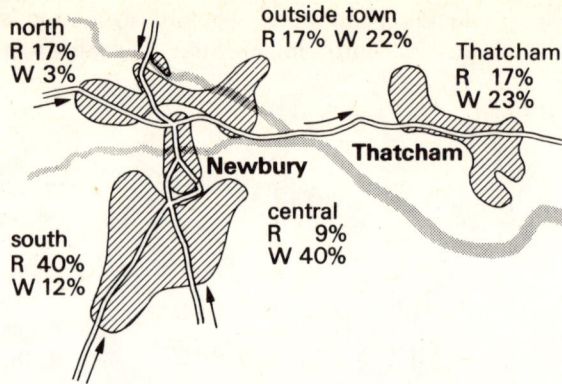

FIGURE 8 *The main zones of traffic generation, showing the percentage of all workers resident in each zone (R), and the percentage of all workers employed in each zone (W). The arrows show the direction of the main traffic flow during the morning rush hour.*

4. Trace or copy Figure 9 into your notebook, and compare it with Figure 7. Read the following paragraph and complete Figure 9 according to the instructions provided.

A proposal for the partial redevelopment of Newbury is shown in Figure 9. Through traffic is removed from the town centre by the provision of an eastern by-pass and a northern by-pass. A local distributor road leaves the eastern by-pass south of the river, runs northwards parallel to Northbook Street, and links up again with the eastern by-pass at two intersections to the west of Victoria Park. This road distributes traffic to various parts of the town, but excludes traffic from the main environmental areas. A multi-storey car park is built over the secondary distributor road in the neighbourhood of North-brook Street, and the new bus station is located immediately to the south of the multi-storey car park. Other car parking areas are provided east and west of Northbrook Street and near the new industrial estate, which is located to the east of the town and south of the river. Oxford Street, Northbrook Street, Bartholomew Street, the Market Place and Cheap Street become a traffic-free pedestrian precinct. A number of pedestrian routes pass under the primary and local distributor roads and link the central precinct with Victoria Park. The business area south of the river is redeveloped with parking and servicing at semi-basement level, ground level shopping and offices above.

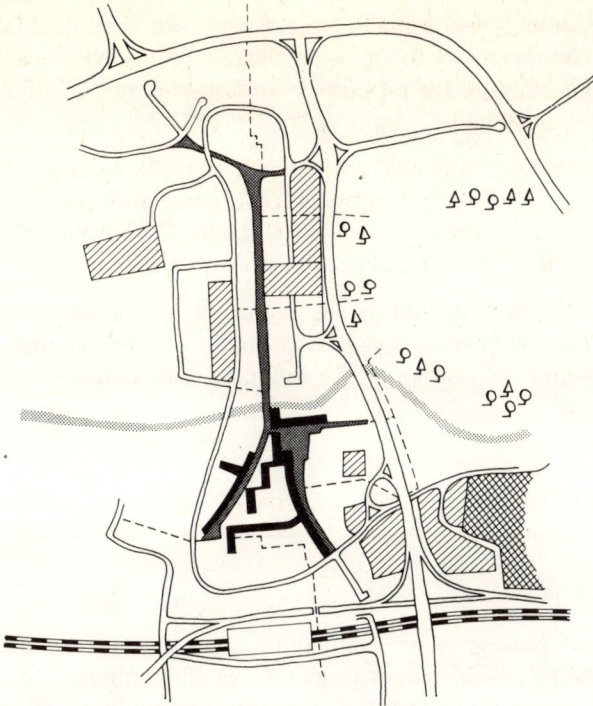

FIGURE 9   *A proposal for the partial redevelopment of Newbury*

Instructions for completing Figure 9

(a) Write labels in the margin with arrows to indicate the following features:

northern by-pass   industrial estate
eastern by-pass   pedestrian route
local distributor road   business area
pedestrian precinct

(b) Add these symbols to the diagram:
P = car park
M = multi-storey car park
B = bus station

(c) Add these labels to the diagram:
Victoria Park   River Kennet
Northbrook Street   Railway Station
Market Place

(d) Indicate route numbers and the direction of the following towns:
A4 to Bath
A4 to London
A34 to Birmingham
A34 to Southampton

5. Using sections 1–4 as a guide, present your own town planning proposal
   based on an imaginary town, or on an actual town which you know well.
   Write an account of the proposal in four paragraphs as follows:

   Paragraph 1: The environs of . . .
   Paragraph 2: Traffic and environmental problems in the central area.
   Paragraph 3: The main zones of traffic generation, and congestion due
                  to work journeys (data may be improvised).
   Paragraph 4: A proposal for the partial redevelopment of . . .

   Each paragraph should be accompanied by a labelled diagram, with
   keys as necessary. You may include material from sections 1–4 above,
   but use your own words where it is appropriate to do so.

III   READING AND NOTE-TAKING

EXERCISE H

The following passage is an unedited extract from the Buchanan Report.*
Read the passage quickly to get a general idea of its contents. Make a note of
any words you do not understand and look them up in a dictionary.

The absorbing interest of the United States is that it has gone more than
twice as far with the motor vehicle as we have in this country.† The ratio
of vehicles per 1000 persons is 410 compared with our own figure of 193.
The total number of vehicles is 75 millions. These figures are reflected
in the powerful impression a visitor receives of a mobile society. The sheer
volumes of traffic, the enormous numbers of cars, the multiplicity of
establishments catering for the needs of motor vehicles and their drivers
and passengers, and the vastness of the engineering works already undertaken, all these make a deep and abiding impression. Yet further large
increases in the numbers of vehicles are anticipated, partly because the
national population is expected to double by the end of the century, and
partly because there is still room for the further intensification of
ownership. Surprising though it may seem, 26% of the families are still
without vehicles, and there are others who would like to have two, three or
even four cars. Already in California joking references are sometimes made
to the 'under-privileged two-car family'.
   There are many differences between conditions in the United States
and in this country which need to be understood if fair deductions are to
be drawn. One of the most important is that there is no statutory land-use
planning system comparable with the highly sophisticated system which

* pp. 180–3.
† i.e. in Britain.

has been evolved in this country. It is not true to say there is no planning, but it does appear to be the case that development largely takes place according to the play of the property market as influenced by the decisions of a very large number of local authorities (many quite small) exercising somewhat elementary zoning powers. The position varies from State to State, but it is said that Houston (Texas), which has grown up without the exercise of any zoning powers at all, is little different from many another American city.

In the absence of any different policy city development has taken the form of sprawl. The sprawl is truly enormous. Greater Philadelphia with a population of 5 millions is already 30 miles across. A journey across Baltimore and then Washington provides nearly 60 miles of unbroken urban development. Los Angeles is 80 miles long, and still growing. The root cause of sprawl is the tremendous population explosion by natural increase, though in California the effect is enhanced by westward migration. The sprawl takes the form that it does primarily because peripheral spread is the 'natural' easy way for a town to expand, and because there has been no effective planning machinery to direct expansion into any other form. But high car ownership, and the post-war mortgage system of the Federal Housing Authority, which has been tied very largely to detached free-standing houses, have powerfully influenced the suburban character of the sprawl.

These enormous spreads of development do not consist only of suburban houses. In the course of time all kinds of development have sprung up – in particular, scattered industry on a big scale, great suburban shopping centres, and major recreational centres such as Disneyland at Los Angeles. This spread and scatter of different activities has, as might be expected, generated cross-currents of movement of the greatest complexity. In many of these metropolitan areas, so great has been the scatter, that the dominating movements are no longer the flow into the centre of the city, but cross-flows between activities on the outer ring. This is especially the case where, as at Los Angeles, there has been a decline in the importance of the central or 'downtown' area.

Initially sprawl starts as a groping for more space for living and for movement and with the belief that, with cars, distance does not really matter – but in the end it produces ever-worsening problems of transportation. The sequence of events is clearly illustrated by Los Angeles which deserves special mention for its claim to have the highest car ownership rate in the world. This enormous conglomeration of development appears to have started as a wide scatter of individual settlements centred on the larger town of Los Angeles itself. In the early days there was an efficient electrified railway linking the settlements. The great expansion of population by immigration then started, and with the motor vehicle then on the scene it produced, as might be expected, a low density spread of development reaching outwards from the old centres. This spread is now roughly

80 miles long and 50 miles wide, but with immigration running at 600 persons per day, it is still expanding.

The electric railway did not long survive the competition of the car, and its end was assisted by the proliferation of level-crossings as development spread out. But eventually the motor vehicle itself began to run into difficulties. The conventional roads along which expansion had taken place became progressively more inadequate for a highly mobile community, and parking problems and congestion in the downtown centre of Los Angeles itself became acute. A 'natural' remedy then began to assert itself. The presence of big suburban populations fostered the growth of suburban shopping and business centres that became highly competitive with the downtown centre on account of the better parking and traffic facilities. The downtown centre suffered considerable loss of business in consequence, and this eventually manifested itself in a visible deterioration of the physical structure, as unprofitable buildings gave way to open parking lots when attempts were made to revive the attractiveness of the centre to the car-owning public. At the same time, however, the construction of an elaborate network of quite new roads – *freeways* as they are called – was commenced with the object of facilitating travel over the length and breadth of the sprawl. This network is now about one-third finished (eventually it will provide a 4-mile grid over the whole area) and already it has greatly facilitated travel, particularly to the downtown area which is enclosed by four tangential roads. Much of the network has had to be built through standing property, and the expense and disturbance have been enormous. That is the position at the moment. It remains to be seen how far the downtown centre will revive itself, and what further development the freeways will themselves stimulate.

Los Angeles prides itself upon being the most motor-minded city on earth. Should it be regarded therefore as a prototype? This is a difficult question to answer. There are places in the Californian sprawl where the workers in the splendid new factories of the 'second industrial revolution' (as the electronic age has been called) live within easy reach of the sea, in houses built to standards far beyond anything we can yet aspire to. There are air-conditioned shopping centres accessible by car, schools, colleges and universities, and a wide range of recreations. If these conditions could be offered to people living in the hard-pressed circumstances of many of our industrial cities, it is difficult to believe they would not grasp them as little short of Utopia. Yet a big doubt remains, for it is impossible to look at Los Angeles as a whole without concluding that had it been the product of deliberate planning, with full powers of land use control, it would have developed quite differently. Almost certainly it would have been made more compact; and one main reason for this, very pertinent to the problem under discussion, is that dispersal taken beyond a certain point complicates the transport situation by positively generating the need for vehicular movement. What Los Angeles does demonstrate is that a big sprawl can function, after a fashion, on the basis of motor transport alone, provided the density of development is not excessive, provided there is only a 'weak' central area permitting the avoidance of the massive traffic flows that a 'strong' centre generates, and provided highway engineering works of the most formidable nature are undertaken. But there is nothing to suggest that we would gain by spreading our own cities out, or still further spreading the conurbations, in order to reproduce the conditions of Los Angeles. All the American experience of sprawl suggests that in our small country we would do well to have no more of it.

EXERCISE I   *Notes*

Now read the passage more slowly and carefully and think about the main points in each paragraph. Make notes as follows:

1. State why the United States is of interest to the town planner.
2. State one important difference between Britain and the United States in the field of town planning.
3. Explain the expression 'urban sprawl', and give three examples. State four reasons for the development of urban sprawl in the United States.
4. How does urban sprawl start? State the sequence of events which led to the present situation in Los Angeles.
5. State some advantages of life in Los Angeles. State one significant disadvantage of urban sprawl. State three conditions that have to be assumed if 'big sprawl' is to function satisfactorily.
6. State the author's conclusion.

DISCUSSION

Re-read the final paragraph of the first reading (p. 95) and consider whether the author's remarks are relevant to a consideration of the traffic problem in any large city that you know.